PINEAPPLE STARS

Sparkling Quilts, Perfectly Pieced

SHARON REXROAD

C&T PUBLISHING

Text © 2005 Sharon Rexroad

Artwork © 2005 C&T Publishing, Inc.

Publisher: Amy Marson

Editorial Director: Gailen Runge

Acquisitions Editor: Jan Grigsby

Developmental Editor: Candie Frankel

Technical Editors: Carolyn Aune, Patricia Wilens, Joyce Engels Lytle

Copyeditor: Stacy Chamness

Proofreader: Wordfirm

Cover Designer: Kristy A. Konitzer

Book Designer/Design Director: Kristy A. Konitzer

Illustrator: Kirstie L. McCormick

Production Assistants: Kerry Graham, Matt Allen

Photography: All flat quilt photographs by Sharon Risedorph except as noted.

All fabric and how-to photographs by C&T staff.

Published by C&T Publishing, Inc., P.O. Box 1456, Lafayette, California, 94549

Front cover: *Springtime Glow* by Sharon Rexroad

Back cover: *School Spirit* and *New Day Dawning* by Sharon Rexroad.

   Oriental Diamond Delight by Janice Lippincott.

Library of Congress Cataloging-in-Publication Data

Rexroad, Sharon.

  Pineapple stars sparkling quilts, perfectly pieced / Sharon Rexroad.

    p. cm.

  Includes index.

  ISBN 1-57120-268-4 (paper trade)

  1. Quilting--Patterns. 2. Patchwork--Patterns. 3. Star quilts. I. Title.

TT835.R45895 2005

746.46'041--dc22

                    2004015851

Printed in China

10 9 8 7 6 5 4 3 2 1

CONTENTS

ABOUT THIS BOOK

In the winter of 1991, I sketched a design that was supposed to be a variation of a Feathered Star quilt. When it was done, I realized that what I had was not a Feathered Star variation, but a diamond-shaped Pineapple block.

I showed the sketch to Mary Bennett, the owner of a local quilt store. Mary was putting together her first schedule of class offerings and said that if I wanted to teach, she would give me the fabric to make the sample. Not one to turn down free fabric, I agreed. The next weekend I figured out how to make the quilt, and two weeks later, I was teaching my first class. Thus began the first of my Pineapple Star designs.

Pineapple Stars offer much to the quiltmaker. In their artistic mode, they encourage us to expand our design vision through effects like color gradation, zinger fabrics, and kaleidoscopic patterns. In the pragmatic world of hands-on sewing, they offer the perfection of paper piecing and the soothing, repetitive rhythms of "doing." This book covers both aspects—the artistic and the practical. Written in a workbook style, it will help you advance quickly from the project quilts to your own creations. I hope you have fun.

To my parents, for teaching me that in life, like in driving, we don't hit detours—we're having an Adventure!

ACKNOWLEDGMENTS

With thanks to my students, who experimented with me along the way and came up with ideas I'd never have thought of on my own; to the quilt guilds that have sponsored my workshops; to Bernina-USA, whose wonderful machines make sewing and quilting a joy, and digitizing and machine embroidery a snap; and to the Nebraska Arts Council, whose early support of my Diamond Pineapple quilts was integral to my development as an artist.

Also, special thanks to Janice Lippincott and Kathy Lichtendahl for sharing their wonderful quilts; to Jan Sears and Linda Huff for their phenomenal machine quilting; to Golden Threads, LLC, and Hari Walner for allowing use of their quilting designs; to Arlene Blackburn for loaning a quilt back for photography; and to the International Quilt Study Center/University of Nebraska and Quilts, Inc., for allowing images of historical quilts from their collections to be included.

Inspiration and Innovation

P ineapple Star quilts take their inspiration from two popular quilt genres. One is the traditional, pieced Pineapple quilt made up of square blocks. The other is the Star of Bethlehem or Lone Star quilt, in which eight 45° diamonds are arranged to form a large central star. In a Pineapple Star, the distinctive pineapple piecing pattern is applied to blocks that are diamond-shaped rather than square.

These new Pineapple Star quilts have several things going for them. The blocks are large, so it doesn't take many of them to fill the quilt center. The pineapple piecing within the blocks adds visual complexity, which in turn makes for a dramatic star when the blocks are put together. Finally, because so many variations are possible, it's hard to get bored.

Studying historical quilts from these two genres heightens my awareness of the design possibilities for my future quiltmaking. I may pull a setting block from an early Star of Bethlehem quilt and combine it with a color flow that I've seen in a Pineapple quilt. The legacy of yesteryear's quilters continually feeds my imagination—I don't think I will ever run out of ideas!

PURRFECTLY SWEET, *Sharon Rexroad, 1992.*

One of my early Diamond Pineapple quilts; second place winner, Crib/Juvenile, National Quilt Festival, Silver Dollar City, 1992

ROSES AMONGST THE THORNS, *Sharon Rexroad, 1995.*

Diamond Pineapple blocks in a Broken Star setting. Second place winner, Bed Quilt/Machine Quilted, and considered for Best Machine Workmanship at the 1996 National Quilting Association show. It is also one of several quilts that garnered me a Nebraska Arts Council Individual Artist Fellowship in the Visual Arts, the first such award given to a Nebraska quilter.

TRADITIONAL PINEAPPLE QUILTS

Classic Pineapple quilts are pieced from square blocks and are similar in feel to Log Cabin quilts. Like Log Cabin blocks, traditional Pineapple blocks start with a square in the center of the block and strips are added in a regular pattern or sequence. In Log Cabin blocks, strips are added to all four sides of a center square; in Pineapple blocks, strips are added on the four sides and diagonally across the four corners as well. The color and texture interaction is rich and complex.

A classic Pineapple quilt's look depends on the fabric choices and whether the blocks are aligned parallel to the edge of the quilt or set on point. Judicious placement of colored fabric strips allows quilters to create patterns across the surface of the quilt or highlight different parts of the quilt.

TRADITIONAL STAR OF BETHLEHEM QUILTS

Star of Bethlehem, or Lone Star, quilts have a more direct impact on my current work. This style of quilt has been documented to the early part of the nineteenth century. The large central star is made up of eight large 45° diamond sections. Each section is composed of a multitude of smaller 45° diamonds. Many of the earliest quilts in this genre use chintz in the setting blocks, either as full pieces of fabric, or cut apart and appliquéd in the *broderie perse* style. In the mid-nineteenth century, quilting or appliquéd flowers were dominant design elements in the setting blocks. By the latter half of the century, pieced stars in the setting blocks were common.

In addition to changes in the setting blocks, the fabric used for the small diamonds also evolved over time. Early Star of Bethlehem quilts used many patterned fabrics. Sometimes these fabrics

PINEAPPLE QUILT, *circa 1870–1890.*

Courtesy of Quilts, Inc. Red and yellow strips halfway through each block result in a secondary design.

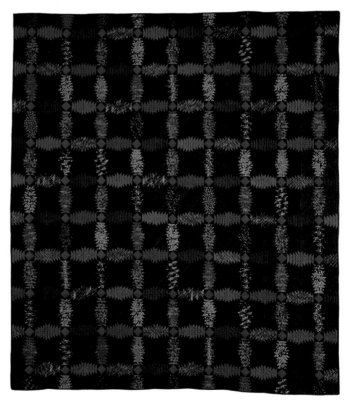

PINEAPPLE QUILT, *circa 1865–1885.*

Courtesy of International Quilt Study Center, University of Nebraska-Lincoln, 1997.007. 0551. The same design looks different using brights and darks and different fabric placement.

STAR OF BETHLEHEM MEDALLION QUILT, *circa 1820–1840.*

Courtesy of International Quilt Study Center, University of Nebraska-Lincoln, 1997.007.0369. Notice the *broderie perse* in the setting blocks and the red star in the center of the quilt.

STAR OF BETHLEHEM QUILT, *circa 1870–1890.*

Courtesy of Quilts, Inc. Notice the use of solid fabrics and extensive quilting.

were busy enough that the small diamonds visually merged, one into another. Later examples from the nineteenth century show a tendency toward solid or subtly patterned fabrics, resulting in clear color definition within the large star. Depending on how the colors and fabrics are placed, classic Star of Bethlehem quilts can feature rings of color, highlighted stars in the center of the quilt, or a "twinkle" effect, achieved by repeating the setting block fabric within the star itself.

Variations on the Star of Bethlehem quilt use more blocks in the design. The most popular of these is the Broken Star setting, in which the central eight-pointed star is surrounded by 45° diamond blocks (32 blocks in all). This style of quilt was particularly popular in the first half of the twentieth century and could be made from a purchased kit. The pastel solids seen in quilts from this era reflect the color sensibilities of the time.

BROKEN STAR QUILT, *circa 1930.*

Courtesy of Quilts, Inc. Notice how the outer blocks use a different color flow than the central blocks to focus attention on an orange LeMoyne Star in the center of the quilt.

FINDING THE RIGHT METHOD

When I first started making Pineapple Star quilts in 1992, I rotary-cut the strips and pieced the blocks assembly-line style. I relied heavily on the 45° angle of a 6" x 24" acrylic grid ruler. This approach proved less than satisfactory. It was difficult for my students to achieve consistent measuring and cutting accuracy. Even minor mistakes became problematic.

Then in the mid to late 1990s came a resurgence of interest in piecing on a paper foundation. I immediately fell in love with the accuracy inherent in paper piecing. It was only a matter of time before I applied foundation piecing to my Pineapple Star blocks. In working out the kinks, I made a small design change to the basic block. My original strip-pieced blocks have a diamond-shaped four-patch in the center. The paper-pieced version features a single diamond instead. The single diamond is more satisfying to me, in part because it better reflects the block's origins as a variation of the Log Cabin block and in part because it adds another design element to the block.

Around this time, I was also discovering how a computer could aid me in my design work. Using Canvas software by Deneba/ACD on a Macintosh computer, I designed my first "computer" Diamond Pineapple block. The software allowed me to generate far more complex designs than I had been able to render with paper and pen.

These various exercises and discoveries came together for me in *Diamond Pineapple #8: Faerie Ring* (page 10), my most complex quilt design to date. For this setting, I merged classic square Pineapple blocks with Diamond Pineapple blocks. The quilt was inspired by a multicolor floral fabric, but I decided to design it in gray-scale. My goal was to refine the value flow and create a luminous effect without having to deal with the impact of color. After a nearly six-month long, nationwide search for the perfect fabrics, I finally began construction of the quilt in the early fall of 1997. The paper piecing alone took a year. The nuances of the color flow required extreme concentration; I could only work on it a week at a time because it was so mentally exhausting. I ended up redoing the first sixteen blocks because the luminous effect wasn't right.

The quilting of *Faerie Ring* involved another redo. Initially, I did the quilting by machine, but I wasn't ecstatic about the results. When the quilt was accepted as a finalist in the "World of Beauty" International Quilt Association contest in Houston in 1998, I decided to take out the machine quilting and hand quilted it with metallic thread instead, in 28 days.

PARADISE STAR, Sharon Rexroad, 1995.

A miniature quilt measuring only 12¹/₂" across, this is my first foundation-pieced Pineapple Star quilt. The quilt won a third place award for Miniatures at the 1996 National Quilting Association show. It has appeared in juried International Quilt Association and American Quilt Society shows.

Diamond Pineapple #8: Faerie Ring, *Sharon Rexroad, 1998.*

An original Diamond Pineapple variation valued for its unique luminous glow. This quilt won a first place ribbon in the Wallhanging/Pieced/Hand-Quilted category at the 1999 National Quilt Association show. It appeared on the cover of *Quilter's Newsletter Magazine* and in various books, magazines, and calendars.

DESIGN

Go With The Flow

THE CLASSIC FABRICATION

A Pineapple Star quilt, in its most basic or classic configuration, is made up of five fabrics. Four of these fabrics are used in the Diamond Pineapple blocks. A fifth fabric is used for the setting blocks.

Put out of your mind any thought that says a star made with just four fabrics will look boring. Some of the most striking quilts use simple fabric combinations. More advanced fabric choices are discussed later in this chapter, but please don't skip ahead. It's important that you understand the classic five-fabric combination before branching out.

Classic four-fabric Diamond Pineapple block

Classic five-fabric Pineapple Star quilt

FOCUS FABRIC

Diamond Pineapple block

The focus fabric appears at the tips of the Diamond Pineapple block. In a Pineapple Star, the focus fabric masses at the center and is repeated at each star point. Because it is so prominent, the focus fabric sets the mood for your quilt. Think of it as your inspiration fabric. The focus fabric can be a floral, a jungle print, a large-scale abstract design—pick your favorite! A heavily patterned or multicolored focus fabric can become a springboard to other fabric choices.

Pay attention to the scale of any print you choose. In a large block, printed motifs can be almost the size of your palm. For a medium block, choose a motif slightly larger than your big toe. For a miniature block, choose something about the size of your thumbnail. You can, of course, go smaller or larger, but for maximum impact, consider using these proportions.

Pineapple Star quilt
Focus fabric

RING FABRIC

Diamond Pineapple block

The ring fabric appears at the broader, "flattened" points of the Diamond Pineapple block. The name is easy to remember; it refers to the ring of color formed halfway out from the center of the Pineapple Star. Think of the ring fabric as the main accent to the focus fabric. A strong accent color in a tone-on-tone or a small-scale print works well. You might also consider using a plaid or a geometric design. If the focus fabric is a floral, using a small plaid or check on the bias for the ring fabric will give your quilt a cottage look.

Pineapple Star quilt
Ring fabric

CRISSCROSS FABRIC

This fabric, as the name implies, crisscrosses the Diamond Pineapple block from edge to edge. On a full Pineapple Star, the crisscross fabric appears in two places—around the star center and close to the outer points. Because it touches both the focus fabric and the ring fabric, the crisscross fabric must not compete with either, but play a supporting role. Less flashy, more subdued colors are typical. If you did not use a geometric for the ring fabric, consider using it here.

Diamond Pineapple block

Pineapple Star quilt
Crisscross fabric

CENTER DIAMOND

The center diamond appears at the middle of the block. If you need a point of reference, think of the classic red or yellow square at the center of a Log Cabin block. The quilt loses visual impact if the center diamond and the crisscross fabric are too close in color or value. Choose something in high contrast to your crisscross fabric to add a punch of color to your quilt. Choose something softer, and the center diamond becomes a calm spot for your eye to rest.

Diamond Pineapple block

Pineapple Star quilt
Center diamond fabric

SETTING BLOCK FABRIC

This fabric is used for the corner squares and side triangles surrounding the Pineapple Star. For a classic look, choose a "pseudo-solid," a small, subtle print. The fabric may be light or dark, depending on the look you are going for and what fabrics are in the star. The setting blocks must be in high contrast to your focus fabric and at least medium contrast to your crisscross fabric. Without contrast, you'll lose the tips of your star (and who wants that?).

Pineapple Star quilt
Setting block fabric

AT THE FABRIC SHOP

How do you find the perfect fabrics for your block? Start by falling in love with a highly patterned inspiration print. This will be your focus fabric. Then find four or five other fabrics that go with it. Take your fabric to a place in the store where you can roll out several yards of each. Don't be shy about asking for such a space. Most stores are happy to oblige.

Follow the steps on these two pages to simulate how the fabrics will appear in a large Diamond Pineapple block. If you are making the medium or miniature block sizes, view smaller sections of fabric.

1. Look at your fabrics and make a preliminary decision as to which fabric might go where in your block.

2. Spread out a yard or so of your potential crisscross fabric. Open up the fabric to its full width.

3. Place a yard of so of your focus fabric on top, so that the crisscross fabric is visible beyond each long edge.

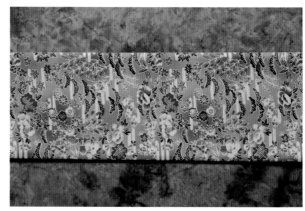

Add focus fabric

4. Fold a yard or so of the ring (main accent) fabric into a lengthwise tube. Lay the ring fabric on top of the focus fabric at a right angle.

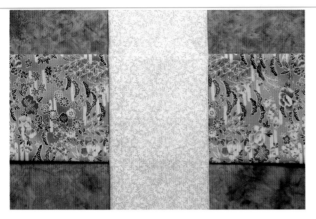

Add ring fabric

5. Fold a fat quarter of the center diamond fabric in half. Scrunch up the ring and focus fabrics where they cross and wrap the center diamond fabric around them. Keep in mind that in an actual block the center diamond fabric touches the crisscross fabric but not the others.

Add center diamond fabric

6. Step back and look at the fabrics. Do you like the colors? The patterns? The balance? If something's not quite right, try switching some of the fabrics. Repeat Steps 1–5 until you arrive at a combination you like. To more closely simulate the look of a Diamond Pineapple block, fold in the loose end of the focus fabric to make a triangle shape.

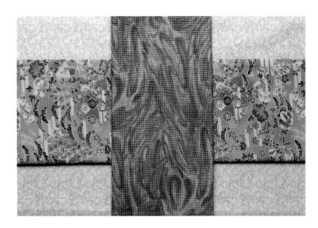

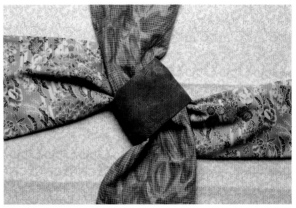

Final arrangement

7. Use the same method to evaluate more advanced color flows.

ADVANCED FABRICATIONS

Classic Fabrication

Feeling adventurous? This next section describes eight subtle (and not-so-subtle!) fabric variations that can add drama to your quilt. For each technique, I pieced a sample block, took a digital photo, and then used my computer software to make a virtual star so that you can see exactly what I am talking about. I used the same focus fabric and general palette for all the examples to help you concentrate on what's unique about each variation.

A word of caution: Don't use more than two or three of these techniques in a single quilt. If you overload the quilt with special features, the design will lose focus.

Interior Zinger Strips

Every Pineapple Star features a mass of focus fabric at the center. To break it up and draw the viewer's eye straight to the star center, you can add a high-contrast zinger strip. Just a little bit of bright, vibrant color near the tip of each block is enough to make the center POP! An interior zinger is especially effective when the center of the quilt is fussy cut.

The technical execution is easy. The zinger strip is sewn in just before the end triangle, in a spot normally occupied by the focus fabric. The zinger option is noted on the paper-piecing pattern in positions 9-S for the four-round blocks and 11-S for the five-round blocks. Make sure you add the zinger fabric at *one end only*. If you add zingers at both ends of the block, they visually cut off the tips and you lose the star effect in your quilt.

Zinger strips

Fussy-Cut Tips

One of the easiest ways to add a little spice to a quilt is to "fussy cut" the focus fabric. You can isolate and display a specific motif at one or both points of the Diamond Pineapple block. If you replicate a single motif eight times and then join those fussy-cut points together, you get a kaleidoscope effect in the center of the Pineapple Star. Using the same or a different motif for the outer star points gives the Pineapple Star its own internal rhythm.

What fabrics fussy cut the best? Prints with a bit of space around the motifs. If the motifs are all mashed together, no matter how interesting they are, the extra work you went to won't matter because the motifs won't show up from a distance. Compare the virtual star at the right with the one below, made with a more densely spaced print, and you'll see what I mean.

Properly spaced tip

Densely spaced print

Densely spaced tip

Fussy-Cut Center Diamonds

The center diamond is a small but key piece in the block. You can make it even more special with a fussy-cut treatment or embellishment. Consider isolating a print motif in your diamond or having the same part of a striped fabric go through the center of every block. In the project quilt *Ribbons & Lace* on page 69, I overlaid the center diamond fabric with a doily. One of my students once surprised me by coming to class with eight small pieces of machine-embroidered fabric. She already had a plan for her center diamonds. Let *your* imagination go wild!

Fussy-cut center diamonds

Interior glow

Interior Glow

Imagine a soft glowing light emanating out of the center of the Pineapple Star. Because the light is low, only the interior of the star is affected. To pull this off, you'll need one light and one dark crisscross fabric from the same color family. Position the lighter strips closer to the end of the block that will become the star center. Position the darker strips at the outer end. You've only added one more fabric to the mix, but the impact is dynamite!

Luminosity

Luminosity is an allover glow. Each block appears to pulsate with its own energy. The glow seems to come toward you, out of the fabric, from someplace deep within the star. It is the most dramatic effect I have discovered so far. To create luminosity, a progression of fabrics—light to dark—take the place of a single crisscross fabric. The lightest fabric is pieced closest to the center diamond. With each round, the crisscross strips become progressively darker.

Choose fabrics for the progression carefully. If you use commercial prints, be sure to compare the fabrics from different distances. What looks like a color progression up close may lose clarity when viewed from across the room. A beautiful (and easy) option is to purchase a gradated set of hand-dyed fat quarters. The project quilt *Springtime Glow* on page 61 uses every other step of an eight-step progression from a purchased collection.

The interplay between all of the fabrics is also critical. The center diamond must be significantly darker than the crisscross fabrics. The focus fabric and ring fabric must contrast with the gradated fabrics. If any of these fabrics blends with the crisscross gradation, the luminescence falls flat. I made this discovery in one of my virtual quilts and made a few thoughtful changes to the block.

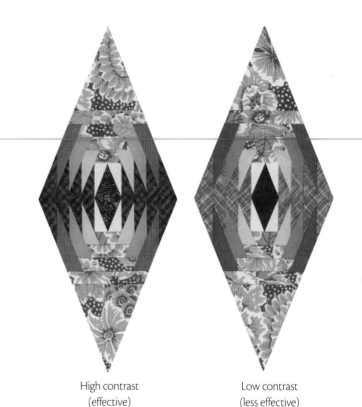

High contrast
(effective)

Low contrast
(less effective)

Luminosity

Low contrast

Rainbowing

Rainbowing

Rainbowing is a gradual change in color family for a specific position in the block. Over the course of four or five rounds, the color might progress from red-orange to red, for example. The increments can be subtle or dramatic. When the blocks are joined in a Pineapple Star, the colors ricochet back and forth within the quilt.

Rainbowing can be applied to any of the major fabric sequences in the block. It is most striking in the ring and crisscross fabrics, which draw the eye around the star rather than out to the points. In the crisscross position, make the colors "rainbow" from one outer edge across the diamond to the opposing outer edge; that is, the rainbow gradation begins at

10-O and ends at 10-I (or, for four-round blocks, 8-O and 8-I). The center diamond acts as a stepping stone in the middle of the color flow. It's a spot of color that contrasts with (but doesn't detract from) the rainbow gradation.

What, exactly, is a "round?" I start counting as soon as I sew a set of four crisscross strips around the center diamond. I add to the count every time I sew on another set of crisscross strips. When I reach the desired number, I sew on the remaining focus and ring fabric pieces until the block is complete.

Companion Print Combos

Lots of fabric collections have companion prints—larger- and smaller-scale fabrics that share colorways and motifs. You can modify the Pineapple Star to showcase them. When you find a combo you like, begin piecing the block as normal, using the smaller-scale print as the focus fabric. When you reach position 9-S for a four-round block or position 11-S for a five-round block, add a zinger strip at one end, and then switch to the larger-scale print for the final end triangle on the same end. Fussy cutting will give this triangle even more zest. In a large block, try one of those great jumbo prints—the ones you normally don't know what to do with—in this spot. If you like how your star turns out, you might want to extend the impact of the companion prints by repeating both of them in the border. Kathy Lichtendahl did this in the project quilt *Butterflies in My Pineapple* on page 73.

Companion prints

Sensational Setting Blocks

Sensational Setting Blocks

Some fabrics are so gorgeous, you can't bear to cut them up. Reserve these beauties for your setting blocks. Examples from the project quilts include the large bouquets in *Ribbons & Lace* on page 69 and the striking hand-dyed *shibori* fabric in *Hothouse Flowers* on page 77.

Like fancy tie-dyeing, *shibori* is Japanese shaped-resist dyeing. The fabric is shaped and secured before it is dyed.

Patterned setting blocks require a rethinking of your other fabric choices. Pay particular attention to the focus fabric; you'll need something subtle and less busy for the star points. For a unique look at the center of the star, replace the focus fabric at the inner tip of the block with a fussy-cut piece of setting block fabric.

Ready, Set, Border!

SPECTACULAR SETTINGS

Diamond Pineapple blocks fit together with geometric precision. There are a variety of settings, ranging from simple to complex. Choosing a setting is like visiting the mix-and-match section of a clothing store. You can put any number of tops together with any number of skirts or slacks. Many combinations are lovely, but one or two are really you!

Star of Bethlehem

Star of Bethlehem is a simple, classic square setting. Eight diamond blocks come together to make an eight-pointed star. Four setting squares and four quarter-square triangles fill in the spaces at the edges. Additional setting fabric can be sewn to the top and bottom edges to extend the design as needed for a bed-size quilt. The project quilt *Hothouse Flowers* on page 77 uses this add-on technique.

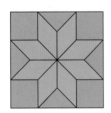

Star of Bethlehem setting

Stretched Star

The Stretched Star setting extends the design internally, without adding extra setting block fabric at the ends. Two three-quarter stars, each made of six diamond blocks, come together in this twelve-block setting. This setting requires four setting squares for the corners and a fifth square, set on point, at the center. Six quarter-square triangles fill in the remaining spaces around the edges.

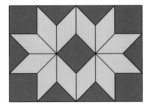

Stretched Star setting

Broken Star

The Broken Star expands on the Star of Bethlehem setting while retaining a square shape. When large diamond blocks are used, the result is a handsome bed-size quilt. A Star of Bethlehem occupies the central position. Each outer tip of this center star touches three more diamond blocks, for 32 diamond blocks in all. The center star is ringed by eight setting squares (four on point). Four more setting squares are paired with four setting rectangles in the L-shaped outer corners. Eight quarter-square triangles fill in the remaining spaces around the edges.

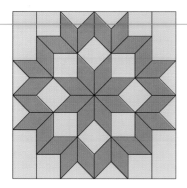

Broken Star setting

Rolling Star

In this variation, a Star of Bethlehem is surrounded by four three-quarter stars. The Rolling Star setting uses the same number of diamonds as the Broken Star, and its finished size is the same. Once you make the blocks, you automatically have two setting options from which to choose.

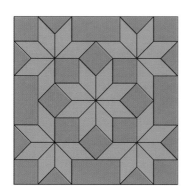

Rolling Star setting

LeMoyne Star Center

When Diamond Pineapple blocks are joined, eight triangles (the block tips) come together at the center of the star. If the triangular block tip is subdivided into diamonds, you get a hint of this design's Star of Bethlehem origins. Subdividing the triangle to make one diamond at the tip produces a single LeMoyne

Star at the center. Subdividing the triangle to make three diamonds adds a second round, for a Double LeMoyne Star.

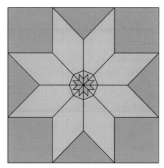
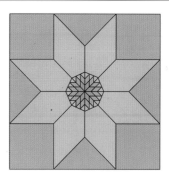

Single LeMoyne Star   Double LeMoyne Star

BRILLIANT BORDERS
Classic Inspiration

The simplest border option is to frame the star with fabrics used in the Diamond Pineapple blocks. A typical combination is to use the ring or zinger fabric in the inner border and the focus fabric in the outer border. Generally, I cut the inner borders the same width as the Diamond Pineapple block piecing strips. You don't need much accent color to make an impact.

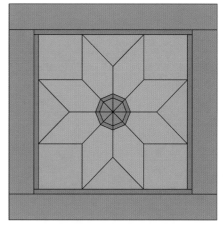

Zinger as an inner border

Pieced Corner Blocks

Pieced blocks in the corners, called cornerstones, add interest to the quilt while retaining the classic look. LeMoyne Stars, Carolina Lilies, and other designs based on 45° diamonds are compatible design choices. Diamonds used in border blocks should correspond roughly in size to the Diamond Pineapple block's center diamond. Choose contrasting colors for the block background and the borders if you want the corner blocks to stand out. If you want the star or lily to "float," like in *Springtime Glow* on page 61, use the same fabric for the block background and borders.

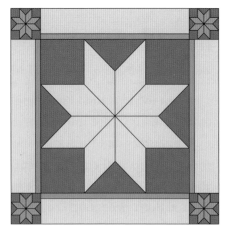

LeMoyne Star corners

LeMoyne Star Border

If you want more stars, you can add them all around the border. Make the stars float, as shown here, by adding inner borders and spacer strips cut from the setting block fabric. For even more interest, you can add spacer strips above and below alternating stars to make the stars move up and down the border. This technique was used in *Hothouse Flowers* on page 77.

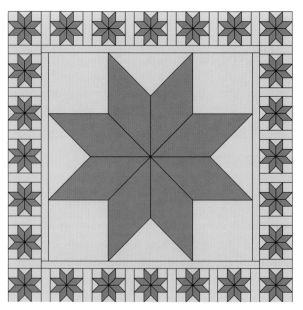

Floating LeMoyne Stars

Binding as the Border

Sometimes, less is more. A simple binding is the classic edge finish for a Broken Star setting; it also works well for a single Pineapple Star. Choose a fabric with high contrast against the setting blocks. The ring, crisscross, or center diamond fabrics are good binding choices for quilts without borders. Narrow piping in the binding seam provides added spark.

Diamond Pineapple Block

BEFORE YOU SEW

All of the Diamond Pineapple blocks in this book are made using paper-piecing patterns. You will need a separate paper pattern for each block you make. Patterns to photocopy are on the pull-out insert. To purchase preprinted patterns, see page 95.

Because I like variety and flexibility in my quilt projects, I've designed the patterns in three different sizes: large, medium, and miniature. Each block pattern has five rounds. A four-round option is indicated on the pattern by dashed lines. The different sections on the pattern are numbered to indicate the piecing order.

BLOCK SIZES

- **LARGE** USED FOR BED QUILTS AND LARGE WALL-HANGINGS. THE PIECED STRIPS ARE ABOUT ⅞" WIDE. A PINEAPPLE STAR FINISHES AT 54¼" (FIVE ROUNDS) OR 45¼" (FOUR ROUNDS).

- **MEDIUM** USED FOR MOST WALLHANGINGS AND ALSO FOR BED-SIZE BROKEN STAR AND ROLLING STAR QUILTS. THE PIECED STRIPS ARE ½" WIDE.

A PINEAPPLE STAR FINISHES AT 29" (FIVE ROUNDS) OR 24⅛" (FOUR ROUNDS).

- **MINIATURE** USED FOR SMALL WALLHANGINGS AND DOLL BED QUILTS. THE PIECED STRIPS ARE ¼" WIDE. A PINEAPPLE STAR FINISHES AT 14½" (FIVE ROUNDS) OR 12" (FOUR ROUNDS).

In addition to the paper pattern, you'll need:

- Rotary cutter (large size with 45 mm wheel works best)

- Quilter's acrylic ruler (24" for large blocks, 18" for medium blocks, 12" for miniatures)

- Self-healing cutting mat

- Add-A-Quarter 12" ruler for large blocks, Add-A-Quarter 6" ruler for medium blocks, Add-An-Eighth 6" ruler for miniature blocks

- 45° Kaleidoscope ruler (optional, but makes certain steps very easy)

- Spray starch (professional or heavy strength), or liquid starch and a spray bottle

- Envelope (long for large and medium blocks, short for miniature blocks)

- Fine pins such as Clover Flower Heads or Iris Fine Silk Pins

STARCH IT!

One of the unexpected supplies for successful paper piecing is starch. Both your rotary cutter and your sewing machine *love* a heavily starched fabric because it reduces the "wobblies"—you know, when the fabric ripples or stretches. You'll love it because you'll achieve more precise piecing and quilting. Starch stabilizes loosely woven fabrics or plaids that you might want to cut on the bias for design purposes.

What kind of starch? Professional-strength spray starch is one option. Another is to make your own solution by mixing two parts liquid starch and three parts water in a spray bottle. Shake the solution and lightly spray your fabrics. Wait a few minutes for the starch to fully absorb into the fibers. Then press with an iron set just below "cotton." Repeat the spraying and pressing sequence. Two light sprayings, instead of one heavy coat, reduce the likelihood of your iron catching on the starch and sticking to the fabric. If you have time, spray the fabric, fold it gently into a plastic bag, and store it in the freezer for an hour or two. You'll be amazed at how easy it is to iron the cold, damp fabric. You can actually leave it in the freezer for a couple of days if life gets busy.

Go easy on the starch if you will be hand quilting. Spray a single pass only, use a more dilute solution (one part starch to three parts water), or skip starching altogether and use spray sizing instead.

CUT THE STRIPS

To prepare the Diamond Pineapple fabrics for piecing, you will cut them into strips and then "subcut" the strips (cut the strips again) into smaller segments. Cutting guides for each project quilt give all the details: which fabric to use, how many strips to cut, how many strips and what sizes to subcut.

As a general rule, strips for large blocks are cut 1¾" wide, strips for medium blocks are cut 1¼" wide, and strips for miniature blocks are cut 1" wide. If you're short on fabric, you can cut your strips ⅛" narrower than these measurements and still have a comfortable piecing allowance.

Make the initial cut on the crosswise grain, from selvage to selvage, unless you have a special reason for doing otherwise. For example, you may want to cut a plaid on the bias, or a stripe on the lengthwise grain, to achieve a particular design effect. A side benefit of cutting plaids on the bias is that it combats any tendencies you might have toward obsessive color and pattern matching.

CUT THE END TRIANGLES

End triangles can be subcut from a strip of fabric using a 45° Kaleidoscope ruler or ordinary rotary cutting tools. Begin by cutting a crosswise strip to the width indicated in the project's cutting guide.

Kaleidoscope-Ruler Method

1. Place the strip right side up. Trim off the selvage at the left edge. Place a 45° Kaleidoscope ruler on top, with the tip of the ruler touching the top edge and the ruler lines parallel to the bottom edge.

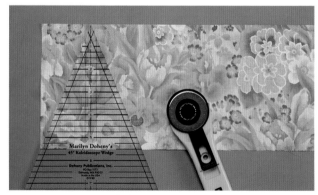

Kaleidoscope-ruler cutting

2. Cut along both angled edges of the ruler with rotary cutter.

3. Rotate the ruler 180°. Align it against the angled cut, with the tip touching the bottom edge of the strip. Make a second cut.

4. Continue rotating the ruler and cutting triangles until you have enough for the project.

Ruler Method

1. Place the strip wrong side up. Trim off the selvage at the left edge.

2. Starting at the left edge, measure and mark the *subcut* measurement (from the block cutting guide) in even increments along the long lower edge. The subcut measurement for triangles is the base of the triangles.

3. Divide the subcut measurement in half. Starting at the left edge, measure and mark this length once on the long top edge.

4. Mark the subcut measurement in even increments along the remainder of the top edge.

Marking

5. Align a quilter's ruler with the first marks on each long edge. Make an angled cut along the ruler's edge.

6. Move the ruler to the right, align it on the next two marks, and make a parallel angled cut. Continue cutting parallelograms across the strip.

7. Subcut each parallelogram in half diagonally to make two triangles.

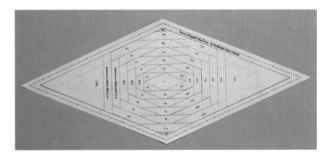

Cutting

PIECING THE BLOCK

1. Trim the paper pattern ½" beyond the seam line (½" past the dotted line on a four-round block).

2. Flip the pattern over, printed side down. Position the center diamond fabric right side up on the plain side of the paper.

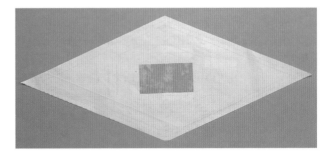

A white work surface will make the printed lines more visible when the pattern is turned face-down. To confirm the fabric alignment before sewing, hold the paper up to a bright light.

3. On the printed side, pin through the paper and fabric. Center the pin between two parallel edges of the diamond. You can also use a light touch of glue from a glue stick to hold the layers together.

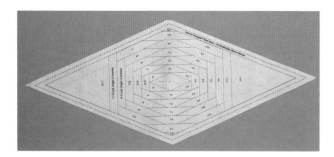

4. On the printed side of the pattern, place the edge of an envelope on a line between positions 1 and 2. The envelope should cover position 1 (the center diamond).

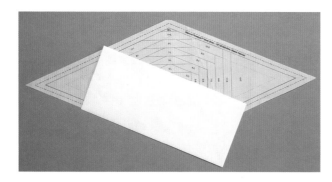

The envelope must always cover the position with the lower number.

5. Fold back the pattern against the edge of the envelope, to make a strong crease on the printed line.

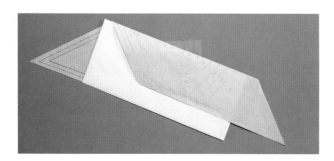

6. Place an Add-A-Quarter or Add-An-Eighth ruler on the pattern so that the lip of the ruler butts up against fold.

7. Run a rotary cutter along the edge of the ruler to trim off the excess fabric.

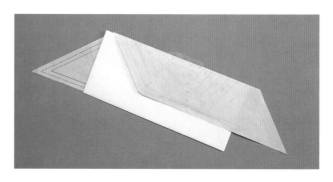

YOU MAY USE A REGULAR QUILTER'S RULER INSTEAD OF AN ADD-A-QUARTER OR ADD-AN-EIGHTH RULER. JUST ALIGN THE RULER'S 1/4" LINE (OR 1/8" MARKS) ON THE FOLD AND CUT ALONG THE RULER EDGE. HOLD THE RULER FIRMLY IN PLACE AS YOU CUT, TO PREVENT SLIPPING.

8. Repeat Steps 4–7 to trim the *opposite* edge of the center diamond. Only cut two edges at this time—one at the base of a position 2-I and one at the base of the opposite position 2-O. Flip the pattern over, fabric side up.

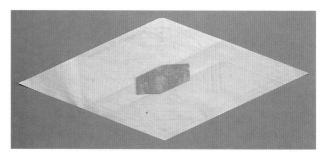

9. Place a crisscross #2 strip on the center diamond fabric, right sides together and raw edges aligned. Pin at both ends. If you are using more than one crisscross fabric, make sure they are positioned appropriately over the pattern. For example, 2-I means "inner" and 2-O means "outer." The position must be taken into account when creating a quilt with Interior Glow.

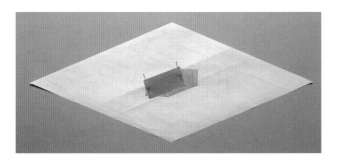

Hold the pattern up to a light source to make sure the stitching line is fully covered by the fabric strip.

10. Flip the pattern over, fabric side down. Stitch on the line at the base of position 2 (the line between 1 and 2). Start stitching three or four stitches *before* the start of line and continue three or four stitches *past* the end of line. Trim off thread ends.

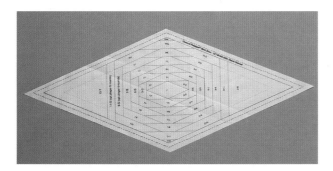

For paper piecing, set the machine to 15 to 18 stitches per inch (1.5 to 2 metric). Test to see if the tip of a tiny seam ripper can get under the stitches.

11. Flip the pattern over, fabric side up. Press the seam flat to anchor the stitches. Then press the fabric strip out.

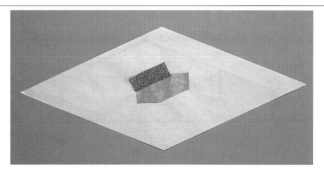

12. Align another crisscross #2 fabric on the opposite trimmed edge of the center diamond. Pin at both ends. Flip over, and sew. Trim thread ends. Flip pattern back with fabric side up and press seam flat, and then press fabric strip out.

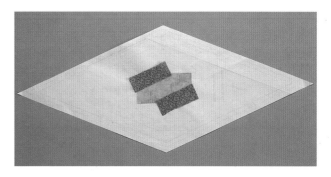

If you're using more than one crisscross fabric, this strip may differ from the first strip.

13. Place the edge of an envelope on one of the remaining position 2 base lines.

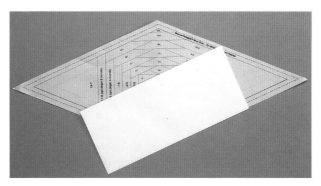

14. Fold back the pattern on the line, against the edge of the envelope, gently tugging the paper loose from the threads at the ends of the seams. Make a sharp crease in the pattern.

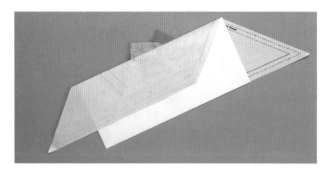

Don't panic if the paper tears a bit as you free it from the previous stitches. You'll still be able to see the pattern lines.

15. Place the "Add-A" ruler on the pattern, butting the lip against the fold. Trim off both the center diamond fabric and the ends of the two strips added in the previous steps.

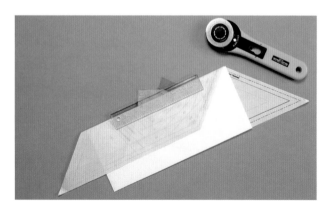

16. Repeat Steps 13–15 to trim the remaining line between positions 1 and 2. Flip the work over, fabric side up.

For easier cutting, use a 45 mm rotary blade or larger. A 28 mm rotary blade isn't deep enough to cut through all the layers.

17. Place one of the remaining two crisscross #2 strips on the center diamond, aligning the raw edges. Make sure to match any special fabric flows with the Inner and Outer #2 positions. Pin in place.

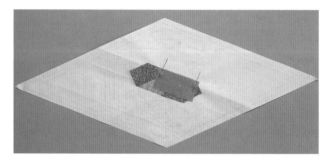

Make sure the ends of the strips cover the diamond edges. Note that the new strips will not extend all the way across the first two strips.

18. Stitch on remaining lines between positions 1 and 2. It's okay to cross the previous stitches. Flip the work over, fabric side up. Press the seams flat to anchor the stitches. Then press the fabric open.

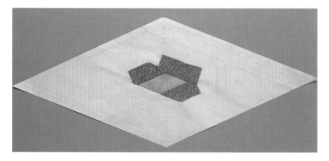

Fine pins reduce the chance that your needle will hit a pin while sewing.

19. Repeat Steps 17 and 18 with the final crisscross #2 fabric strip.

20. Flip the pattern over, fabric side down. Position the envelope on a long line between positions 2 and 3-L. Fold back on line, against the envelope, loosening stitches as needed. Make a sharp crease in the pattern. Place a ruler on the pattern, butting the lip up against the crease. Trim fabric. Repeat to trim the remaining long position 3-L.

21. Flip the pattern over, fabric side up.

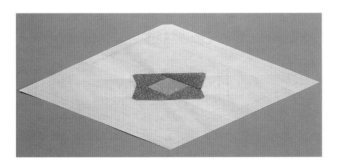

Trim and sew each long position before doing the short ones. Continue this pattern for the rest of the block. To remember the sequence, think of the phrase "the long and the short of it."

22. Fold a ring #3-L strip in half, right side out. Place it on the block, raw edges matching. Align the folded edge with a wide point of the center diamond.

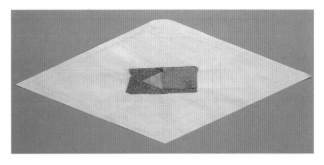

23. Unfold the strip so the fabrics are right sides together. Pin at both ends.

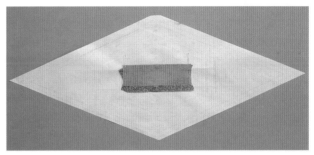

24. Flip the pattern over, printed side up. Stitch on long line at base of position 3-L. Flip the pattern over, fabric side up. Press the seam flat, then press the fabric open.

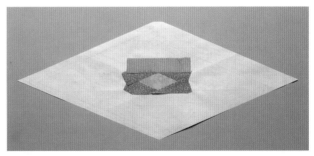

25. Repeat Steps 21–24 with the remaining ring #3-L strip.

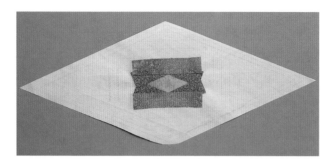

If you make a mistake, don't go wild with your seam ripper. Working on the fabric side of the block, carefully slip the tip under every fifth or sixth stitch and break the thread. Then flip the pattern over to the paper side and loosen one section. Once you get it started, the rest of the thread should pull out without too much trouble.

26. Flip the pattern over, fabric side down. Position the envelope on a *short* line between positions 2 and 3-S. Fold back on line, against the envelope, loosening stitches as needed. Make a sharp crease in the pattern. Place a ruler on the pattern, butting the lip up against the crease. Trim fabric. Repeat to trim the remaining short position 3-S.

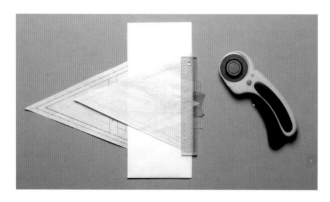

27. Flip the pattern over, fabric side up.

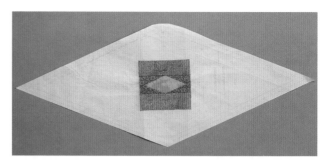

28. Align a focus #3 strip on each short trimmed edge, right sides together. Pin at both ends.

29. Flip the pattern over, printed side up. Stitch on both short lines at base of position 3. Flip the pattern over, fabric side up. Press the seams flat, then press the fabric open.

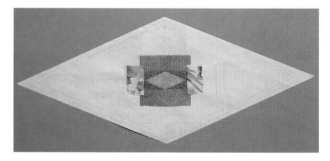

30. Flip the pattern over, fabric side down. Position the envelope along the base of position 4. Fold back on line, against the envelope, loosening stitches as needed. Make a sharp crease in the pattern. Place a ruler on the pattern, butting the lip up against the crease. Trim fabric. Repeat to trim the diagonally opposite position 4 edge. Flip the pattern over, fabric side up.

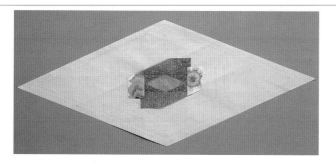

31. Align a crisscross #4 strip on each trimmed edge, right sides together. Pin at both ends. Flip the pattern over, printed side up. Stitch on both short lines at base of position 4. Flip the pattern over, fabric side up. Press the seams flat, then press the fabric open.

32. Repeat Steps 13–15 to trim the remaining two position 4 edges.

33. Repeat Step 31 to add the remaining two crisscross #4 strips.

34. Repeat Steps 20–21 to trim the long edges between positions 4 and 5-L.

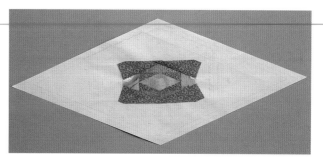

35. Repeat Steps 22–25 to add two ring #5-L strips.

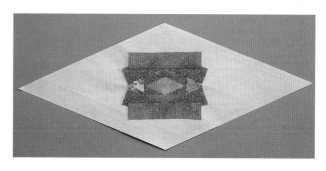

36. Repeat Steps 26–27 to trim the short edges between positions 4 and 5-S.

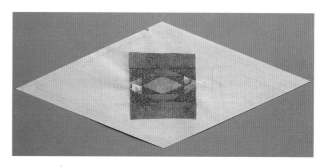

37. Repeat Steps 28–29 to add two focus #5-S strips.

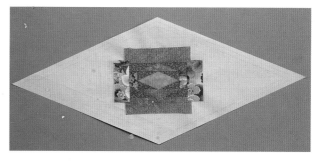

38. Repeat Steps 30–34 to add four crisscross #6 strips.

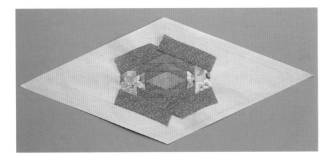

39. Repeat Steps 22–27 to add two ring #7-L strips. Repeat Steps 28–30 to add two focus #7-S strips.

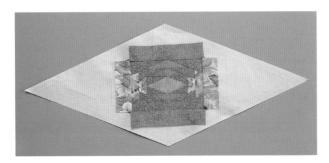

40. Continue the established pattern, adding the crisscross #8, ring #9-L, focus #9-S, and crisscross #10 strips.

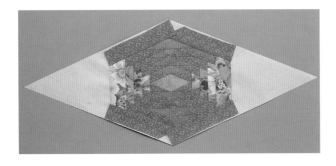

IN A FOUR-ROUND BLOCK, THERE ARE NO CRISS-CROSS #10 STRIPS—THE LAST CRISSCROSS STRIP IS #8. IF THERE IS AN INTERIOR ZINGER FABRIC, IT OCCUPIES ONE OF THE 9-S POSITIONS. USE THE RULER TO TRIM THE EDGES OF RING 9-L AND THE FOCUS (OR ZINGER) #9-S STRIPS.

41. For a five-round block, add the ring #11-L and focus #11-S strips. For a five-round block with an interior zinger, place the zinger fabric strip in one of the #11-S positions as marked on the pattern. Use the ruler to trim the edges of ring #11-L and the focus (or zinger) #11-S strips. Note that there is no position 12 on the pattern. The crisscross sequence ends with position 10.

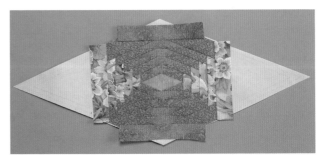

42. Place the ring #13-L strips and the focus #13 triangles at each end of the block. If you fussy cut the end triangles, this is a good time to double-check the pattern placement.

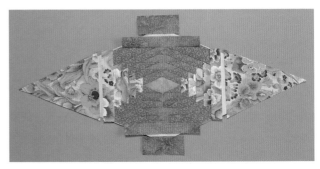

43. Align each #13 triangle on the adjacent focus #11-S strip, right sides together. Pin at both ends of seam line. Center each ring #13-L strip on the adjacent #11-S strip, right sides together. Pin at both ends of the seam line.

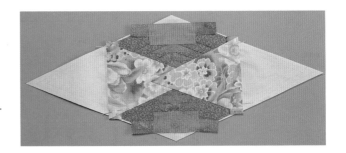

44. Flip the pattern over, printed side up. Stitch on the lines at the base of the position 13 triangles and at base of tiny 13-L triangles. Flip the pattern over, fabric side up. Press the seams flat, then press the fabric open. Pin the triangle tips to the paper.

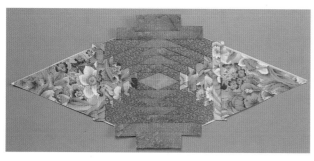

Handle the end triangles carefully during piecing and pressing. Be careful not to stretch the bias cut edges.

45. Flip the pattern over, printed side up. Machine-baste in the middle of the seam allowance, or about ⅛" from the seam line. Don't worry if the stitching isn't perfect. Extreme precision is not necessary. Begin a new line of stitching on each side.

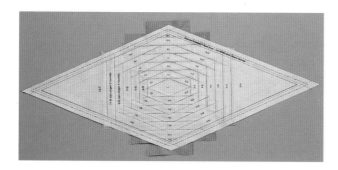

It's very important that each block edge be basted separately. You'll create problems down the line when it's time to remove the stitches if you take a shortcut by pivoting and turning at the corners.

46. Use your rotary cutter and regular quilter's ruler to trim the edges of the block ¼" outside the seam-lines. Flip the block over and admire your work!

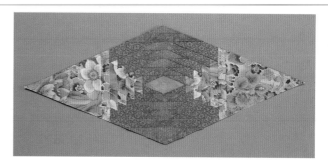

FANCYING UP THE BLOCK

CENTER DIAMOND

The center diamond—position 1—is a great place to showcase a motif, stripe, or geometric design. To better visualize potential motifs in your fabric, make a window with your hands.

- For large blocks, stretch out and align the thumbs and index fingers tip to tip, in a diamond shape.

- For medium blocks, join the tips of a thumb and index finger in an oval.

- For miniature blocks, roll up an index finger and press the top joint against the base of the thumb.

THE CENTER OF THE STAR

The center of the star, where all eight blocks come together, is another good place to heighten the visual drama. The intensity created by a symmetrical, rotating, or spinning repeat at this location cannot be underestimated. A zinger strip at the base of the triangle ups the ante.

To create the effect, you will need to isolate a motif, stripe, or other design for the triangle and then cut one triangle per block. A basic Pineapple Star quilt requires eight triangles. A Broken Star setting requires eight triangles for the center star plus four sets of three and four sets of two for the outer part of the design. You'll use a paper window template to audition potential motifs and a triangle template to cut the pieces.

1. Photocopy the triangle end of the block pattern. Using a rotary cutter and ruler, cut on the seam line and remove the triangle. Place the window template on the fabric. Rotate it and move it around to isolate possible motifs. When you find a motif you like, pin the window template to the fabric.

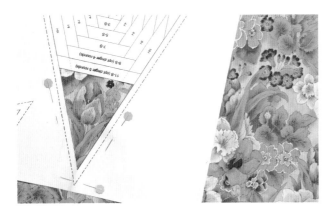

2. Make 8 photocopies of the motif. Cut out the photocopied triangles and tape them together. If you like the design, great! If not, repeat the audition process.

3. Once a motif has your approval, place the triangle cutout back into the window opening. Pin it in place.

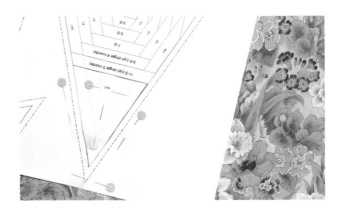

4. Unpin and remove the window template, leaving just the triangle. Use a quilter's ruler to add a ¼" seam allowance (large and medium blocks) or a ⅛" seam allowance (miniature blocks) to the base of the triangle. Cut with a rotary cutter.

5. Add a ½" seam allowance to the two remaining edges. Cut out the triangle.

6. Use the fabric triangle as a template to cut out the next motif. Place the triangle on the appropriate spot on the fabric, matching the designs at the edges. Cut out the new triangle. Repeat until you have cut the required number of triangles. Add the triangles to the block as described in Piecing the Block, Steps 42–46, on pages 34–35.

LeMoyne Star Center

A LeMoyne Star at the center of the Pineapple Star, described on page 23, is made by sewing a pieced triangle to the end of the diamond block. In a five-round block, this pieced triangle takes the place of the 13-T end triangle. In a four-round block, you'll replace the 11-S end triangle to make a single LeMoyne Star and the 9-S position and 11-S end triangle to make a double LeMoyne Star. Template patterns for all of these variations in all three block sizes are on the pattern insert. Cut the required number of pieces for your quilt setting.

♦ **Single LeMoyne Star.** Arrange pieces A, B, and C as shown. Sew A to B. Press seam open. Join AB to C. Press seam open. Repeat for each block.

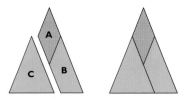

Single LeMoyne tip

♦ **Double LeMoyne Star.** Arrange 1 A1, 2 A2's, and 3 D's, as shown. Sew the pieces together in diagonal rows. Press seams open. Join the rows. Press seams open. Repeat for each block.

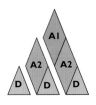

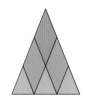

Double LeMoyne tip

Add the triangle to the block as described in Piecing the Block, Steps 42–46, on pages 34–35.

Piecing the Star

Your Diamond Pineapple blocks are pieced. Congratulations! The time-consuming part is done. The next step is to sew eight blocks together to make a Pineapple Star. In more complex quilt settings, blocks are joined into smaller units as well. The same piecing method applies.

Remove all but the last three rounds of the paper pattern from each block. Less paper makes the blocks more flexible and easier to handle when piecing the blocks together. It also gives you a head start on the inevitable paper-removal chore at the end of the project. That's when you want to spend time celebrating, not tearing out paper!

I find it easier to remove papers if I've gently tugged on the blocks in a couple of directions before starting the removal process—it seems to break the fibers in the paper underneath stitches. I also run a seam ripper, dull side down, along the stitching line to further weaken the paper. After tearing off the paper, use the tip of the seam ripper or the tip of a pin or a used machine needle to get out any remaining paper fibers. Bits of paper tend to get stuck where seams cross.

PINNING PAIRS

How do you get all the angles in the Diamond Pineapple blocks to match across seamlines? The answer is, in a word, pin. I know it's out of vogue to pin much in today's quilt world, and there are lots of times I don't pin. But you'll have to trust me on this one. The accuracy afforded by pinning is worth the extra effort when it comes to Pineapple Stars.

I must also convince you of the importance of using *two* pins at each join: a "matching" pin, inserted vertically through critical intersections, and a "holding" pin, inserted horizontally to hold the layers together. Take this extra step and you'll rarely have to redo seams because the match is off. I know you'll like that part.

1. Layer two blocks right sides together, with the tip of the blocks at the upper right and the edges to be sewn to the right. You'll pin the broader point first and move toward the tip.

2. Insert a pin vertically into the seamline *exactly* at the broader point. Go through the paper and fabric of the top block and then through the fabric and paper of the lower block. Flip the block over and verify that the pin comes out exactly on the broad point seamline. This pin is the matching pin.

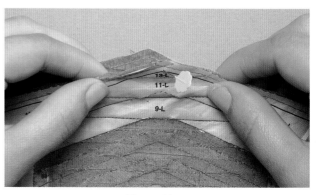

Top position

and paper of the bottom block. Flip the block over and verify that the pin comes out exactly where the seamlines intersect.

3. Keep the matching pin in a vertical position. Pinch the papers together close to the pin, as shown, to make the alignment perfect.

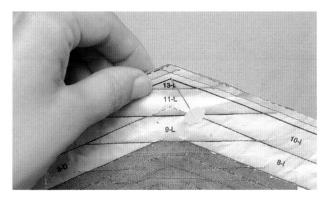

Pinch to align

4. Slip the tip of a second pin *between* the top paper and the wrong side of the fabric of the top block, as shown. I know it feels awkward, but by pinning through the fabric layer first, instead of the paper, your blocks are less likely to shift and your matches will be more accurate. Push the pin through the bottom block and then back up through top block. Remove the matching pin. The pin that remains is the holding pin.

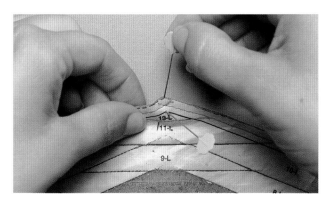

The holding pin goes in

5. Make the next match on the seamline exactly where the ring and crisscross fabrics come together. Insert a vertical matching pin through the paper and fabric of the top block and then through the fabric

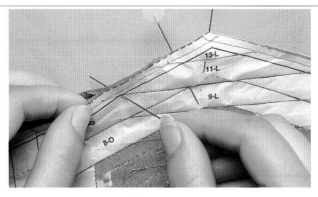

New matching pin

6. Repeat Steps 3 and 4 to pin the layers together. Remember to remove the matching pin. Pin the next intersection, where the crisscross and focus fabrics come together, in the same way.

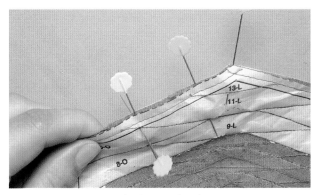

Pinning completed

7. Insert a matching pin vertically through tips of triangles. Add a second pin horizontally.

Pin the tips

To match fussy-cut end triangles, pick a spot on the motif. Go through the same spot each time you pin.

8. Make one more match at the middle of the long edge of end triangle. Pin as before.

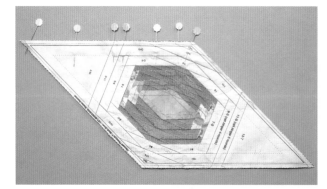

Final matching pin

SEWING PAIRS

1. Set the machine for a short stitch length, from 15 to 18 stitches per inch (or 1.5 to 2 metric). Begin *off* the edge of the block. Sew the pinned seamline, from the triangle end toward the broad tip.

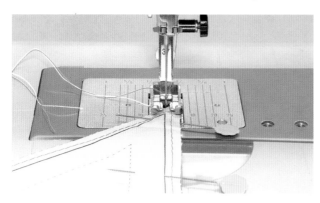

Ready to sew

2. As you reach the end of the seamline, slow down. Stop exactly at the printed seamlines at the broad point, with the needle in the down position. Do not sew off the end of the block.

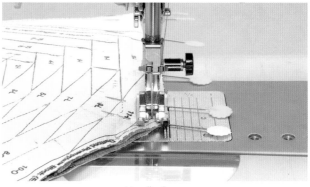

Needle down

3. Backstitch about ½". Release the presser foot, clip the threads, and remove the blocks from the machine.

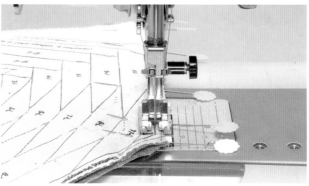

Backstitch

4. Open up the blocks. Check the accuracy of the seam matches. Make sure special motifs come together as planned.

Check the seam matches

5. Remove the basting stitches from both seam allowances of the seam just sewn. Gently tear off the paper from both seam allowances. Tear off and remove the paper close to the just sewn seam. Leave the paper in place near other edges of block.

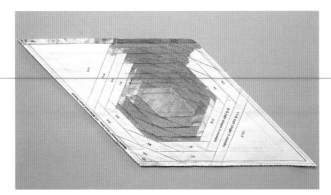

Paper removal

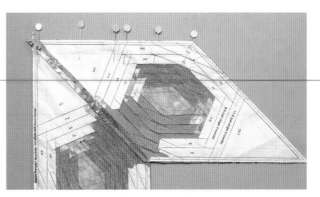

Pin the tips

6. Gently press the seam open on the wrong side of the blocks. Press again on the right side.

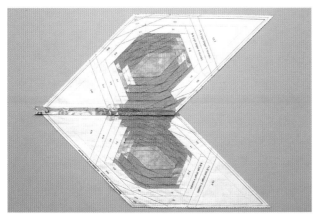

Seam pressed open

If you prefer, do not trim the dog ears left by the tips of the triangles until after the next cross seam is sewn. They will give you something to hold onto if you need to tweak the seams into a perfect match.

SEWING A HALF-STAR

1. Layer two Diamond Pineapple pairs right sides together, with the edge to be pinned on the right. Match and pin the edges together, as for two single blocks. When you reach the spot where the four tips come together, insert the matching pin through the valleys of the already sewn seams.

Tear an inch of paper off the tip of each block right before pinning. By removing it now, you won't have to use tweezers to pick out tiny bits of paper from the sewn seams.

2. Repeat Sewing Pairs, Steps 1–4, to join the blocks together.

3. Repeat Sewing Pairs, Steps 5–6, to examine and press the seam. Trim the dog ears from the right edge of the just sewn seam. Leave the tips which point vertically.

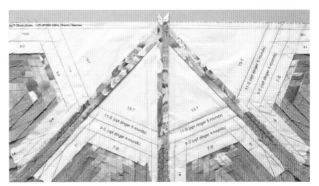

Press seam open

SEWING A FULL STAR

1. Layer two star halves, right sides together, with the edge to be pinned on the right. Match and pin the edges, beginning at the lower flattened corner. When you reach the star center, insert a matching pin at the little V-shaped intersection of the previous seams. Check the underside to see that the pin emerges at the V.

Pin at the V

2. Pinch the layers together to stabilize the match. Insert horizontal pins just before and after the match. Remove the vertical matching pin. Add one last pin 1½" past the center match pins.

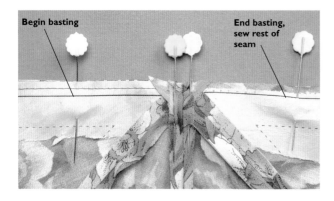

Begin basting

End basting, sew rest of seam

3. Set the machine to 8 stitches per inch (3.5 metric). Beginning 1" before center match, machine-baste the layers together. When you have sewn 1" past the center match, reset the machine to 15 to 18 stitches per inch (1.5 to 2 metric). Sew the rest of the pinned seam, backstitching at the end.

Ready to sew

4. Open up the partially sewn seam. Check the matches, especially where the eight blocks come together. If necessary, take out the basting stitches and redo the center match.

Check the match

5. Match and pin the remainder of the seam, as in Step 1. Set the machine to 15 to 18 stitches per inch (1.5 to 2 metric). Sew over the basting stitches at the center seam. Continue sewing the entire seam, stopping and backstitching when you reach the end of the seamline. Open the star and check the matches. Remove the basting stitches and paper from both seam allowances. Remove the paper close to the just sewn seam. Leave the paper around the star edges in place. Trim the remaining dog ears. Press the seam open on the wrong side.

Press seams from the wrong side

6. Flip to the fabric side, lay a press cloth over the center star and press again on the right side. Step back and admire your star!

A "volcano" at the center of the star means you've stretched the bias edges of the fabrics. Steam the volcano with an iron and pat it down by hand. Apply a shot of spray starch. Lay a press cloth over the top and press flat. Let the fabric cool completely before removing it from the ironing surface.

OTHER BLOCK COMBINATIONS

In more complex quilt settings, resist the natural inclination to piece many Diamond Pineapple blocks together at one time. To facilitate the setting block insertions, only partial star units are assembled. The Stretched Star variation, for example, looks like two three-quarter stars joined together, but that's not how the blocks are prepared. Follow the sequences illustrated below before you move on to joining setting pieces as described in the next section. Consult the basic star piecing instructions at the beginning of this chapter as needed.

STRETCHED STAR

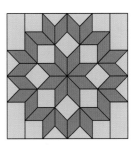

Stretched Star setting

1. Arrange 12 Diamond Pineapple blocks as they appear in the Stretched Star setting.

2. Piece the blocks together in pairs. Press open. Make 6 pairs.

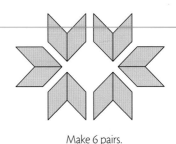

Make 6 pairs.

3. Join 4 pairs to make 2 half-stars. Press open.

4. Join the remaining 2 pairs in a horizontal sequence that resembles rickrack. Sew from the triangle tips toward the broader tip. Stop and backstitch at the end of the stitching line. Press the seam as usual.

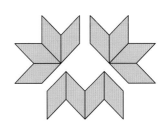

Stretched Star assembly

BROKEN STAR

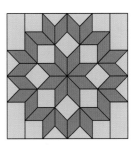

Broken Star setting

1. Arrange 32 Diamond Pineapple blocks as they appear in the Broken Star setting. Make sure blocks with advanced fabrications (such as zinger strips or interior glow) are properly positioned for the desired result.

2. Piece the blocks together in pairs. Press open. Make 16 pairs. Note that 4 pairs (the ones that point to the corners of the quilt) are joined at the outer tips instead of the inner tips. If the blocks have an advanced fabrication, these pairs will look different from the others.

Make 16 pairs.

3. Make 2 half-stars. Press open. Join them to complete the center star.

4. Join 2 pairs at the top in a horizontal sequence that resembles rickrack. Sew from the triangle tips toward the broader tip. Stop and backstitch at the end of the stitching line. Press the seam as usual. Make 4 rickrack units, one for each edge of the quilt top.

Broken Star assembly

ROLLING STAR

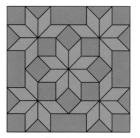

Rolling Star setting

1. Arrange 32 Diamond Pineapple blocks as they appear in the Rolling Star setting. Make sure blocks with advanced fabrications (such as zinger strips or interior glow) are properly positioned for the desired result.

2. Piece the center star blocks and four blocks at each corner together in pairs. Make 12 pairs. Press open. The eight blocks that touch the tips of the center star do not get sewn until the setting block stage.

Make 12 pairs.

3. Make 2 half-stars for the center block. Press seams as usual. Join them to complete the center star. Make 1 half-star for each corner.

Rolling Star assembly

TECHNIQUE

Setting Blocks

Setting blocks play an essential role. They link the Diamond Pineapple blocks in a quilt. In a traditional Pineapple Star quilt, they fill in the gaps at the corners and around the edges of the center star. In more complex quilts, they occupy interior spots as well. Because we are using diamond-shaped blocks, the piecing is a little more involved than simply sewing blocks together in rows. This chapter explains how to prepare the blocks and connect them to the paper-pieced diamonds.

THE GRAIN THING

You already know how to cut squares and rectangles. The only thing I have to add is to pay attention to the fabric grain. When a special fabric, like a floral chintz or a stripe, is used for the setting squares, it's pretty obvious whether or not the pattern is going in the right direction. What is not immediately obvious is that issues of grain and pattern can flare up even in quiet fabrics. There may be a hidden pattern or stripe that you don't see up close, but that becomes apparent when you step back and view the quilt from across the room. The way light reflects off a solid fabric may depend on which way the fabric is turned.

Keeping the grain of the setting blocks consistent is important to the success of a finished quilt. A wallhanging hangs straighter if the lengthwise grain (the grain that runs parallel to the selvage) runs vertically in the quilt. As soon as you cut a setting block, mark the lengthwise grain on the back with a pencil or a piece of tape so that you can keep all of your setting blocks on track.

Sometimes setting squares end up on point. These squares can be cut on grain or on the bias. If you opt for a bias cut—to keep a pattern upright in the quilt, for instance—stabilize the fabric with starch before you cut it.

It is also important that the long edges of setting triangles be on grain. If they aren't, the edges of the finished quilt will wave. Cutting quarter-square triangles (as opposed to half-square triangles) prevents this from happening. To make four setting triangles, cut one large square. Then subcut the square diagonally in both directions. Two of the triangles will have the lengthwise grain running parallel to the long edge. The other two will have the lengthwise grain running perpendicular to the long edge. Mark which is which, and you'll be able to keep the setting triangles in sync.

Quarter-Square Triangles

To make sure nothing goes wrong in the grain department as you do the final assembly, lay out all the Diamond Pineapple blocks and setting blocks on a design wall or the floor. Arrange the setting blocks so that the lengthwise grain runs consistently in the same direction. Immediately after sewing units together, physically return them to the layout to verify how they will be joined to the remaining pieces.

Y-SEAMS MADE EASY

All Pineapple Star quilts use set-in Y-seams to add the setting blocks. I'll share my favorite method for sewing a Y-seam. But first, make sure your star seams stop ¼" from the block edges. Revisit Sewing Pairs, Steps 2–4, on page 40. Did you remember to stop at the end of the sewing line and backstitch instead of continuing off the edge? Second, it helps if the seams are pressed open, both for the Y-seam construction and to make your quilt lie flat.

1. Place the setting square right side up, with the corner that is being inserted in the Y-seam at the lower right. Insert a pin into the lower right corner, ¼" in from both edges.

Pin ¹/₄" from corner

2. Place the pieced star on the square, right sides together, so the pin is inside the Y opening, butting right up to where the stitching stops.

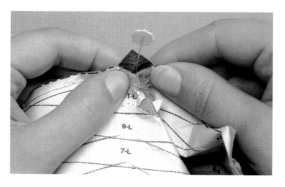

Pin the Y opening

3. Using the pin as a pivot point, rotate the star until the first edge to be sewn is aligned with right edge of the square and the second edge to be sewn extends past the square at the lower right. Make sure the Y opening remains butted up to the pin. Pin the edges to be sewn; insert the first pin directly above the pivot pin, the second pin at the top of the seam by the tip of the star, then fill in between. Starting at the edge of the fabric, sew from the top of the seam toward the Y, slowing down as you approach it.

Sew toward the Y

At the top of the seam, remember to match the actual seam position (¼" in from edges) and not the outer edges of the pieces being joined. This is especially critical when joining squares, diamonds, and triangles, as the edges don't match.

4. When you reach the Y, take one stitch into the opening itself, going through the setting square fabric only (not through the star). Leave the needle in the fabric. The needle should be exactly at the ¼" mark, where the pivoting pin was. Raise the presser foot, but leave the needle down.

Needle down, presser foot up

5. Remove any pins that remain in the first seam. Lift up the pieced star and gently grab the bottom layer of fabric (the setting square). Using the needle as a pivot point, rotate this fabric until the next edge to be sewn is directly in front of the needle.

Pivot the setting block

6. Rotate the top layer (the Pineapple Star) in the opposite direction until the next edge to be sewn is aligned with the bottom layer. Make sure that the Y opening is butted up to the needle. Pin along the

next seam, matching the ends. Lower the presser foot and carefully begin stitching the seam. Continue off the edge of the fabric.

Pivot the Pineapple Star

7. Remove any remaining paper in the vicinity of the two seams. Press seams open.

If you want the setting blocks to physically recede behind the star, press the seam allowances toward the star.

SEWING THE SETTINGS

Refer to Y-Seams Made Easy to sew the following settings.

STAR OF BETHLEHEM

In this basic setting, the triangles are inserted before the squares. This sequence allows you to match the edges of the quilt top as well as the seam lines when inserting the setting blocks.

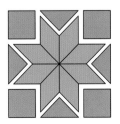

Setting blocks layout

1. Insert a setting triangle at each edge of the star.

2. Insert a setting square at each corner.

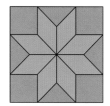

Star of Bethlehem

STRETCHED STAR

Once you get beyond the basic Star of Bethlehem arrangement, the assembly sequence becomes a bit more involved. In a Stretched Star arrangement, the quilt has three major sections. Each section is pieced individually. Then all three sections are joined together. Two remaining setting squares are added last.

1. Insert 2 setting triangles and 1 setting square into the rickrack unit and into each half-star.

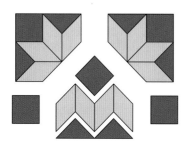

Setting blocks layout

2. Join the half-star units together. At the wider star points, backstitch at the end of the seamline to facilitate the next Y-seam.

3. Sew a large Y-seam to join the three units. Be sure to match the center intersection of each half-star to the rickrack unit as you pin and sew.

Remember to backstitch at both the beginning and end of the Y-seam to facilitate insertion of remaining setting squares.

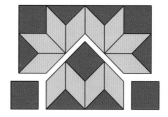

Partial assembly

4. Insert setting squares at the lower left and lower right corners.

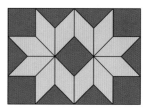

Stretched Star

BROKEN STAR

I work this complex setting from the inside out. Smaller Y-seams are sewn first, to complete the outside units and transform the center star into a large X shape. When I sew the large Y-seams, the design really begins to come together. The corners are added last.

1. Insert 1 setting square and 2 setting triangles into each rickrack unit.

2. Insert 1 setting square into each 2-block unit. Begin and end the seam by stitching off the blocks.

Stretched Star assembly

3. Join the units from Step 2 to the star to make a large X-shaped unit. Begin and end each seam by stitching off the blocks.

Partial assembly

4. Insert 4 rickrack units into the large X unit. Be sure to match the seams of the block tips as you pin and sew. Remember to backstitch at the beginning and end of each large Y-seam.

5. Insert 4 setting squares at the top and bottom edges.

6. Insert 4 setting rectangles to complete the L-shaped corners.

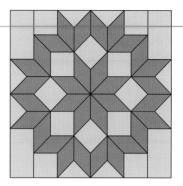

Broken Star

ROLLING STAR

Rolling Star is the most technically difficult of the Pineapple Star arrangements in this book. To insert the "lazy" diamonds, you'll use a wide Y-seam construction. I call them lazy diamonds because the blocks appear to be lying down.

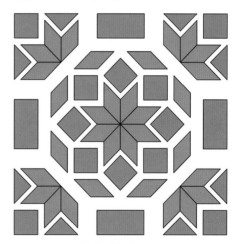

Setting block layout

1. Insert 1 setting square and 2 setting triangles into each half-star unit. Sew off the edges of the blocks.

2. Insert a setting square into the center star, backstitching at the beginning and end of the sewing line.

3. Finger-press the seam toward the setting block. Pin the next setting block in place, matching the ends of the sewing lines, and stitch as before. Be careful not to catch the previous seam in the stitching. Repeat until 8 setting squares are inserted.

Backstitch at the end of the sewing line.

4. Insert the wider point of a lazy Diamond Pineapple block into the wide Y opening of two setting squares in the center star unit. Use the same pinning and stitching method as for a Y-seam, except start with the Diamond Pineapple block right side up and the setting squares right side down. When you get to the pivot point, push the tip of the original Diamond Pineapple block (the one that is part of the star) out of the way so that it does not get caught up in the stitching. Begin and end your stitching lines by sewing off the edge of the lazy Diamond Pineapple blocks. Repeat until 8 lazy diamonds are inserted.

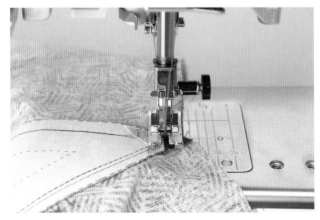

Approach pivot

After pivot

5. Join the half-star corner units to the diagonal edges of the center star unit, backstitching at beginning and end of each seam. Press the seams open.

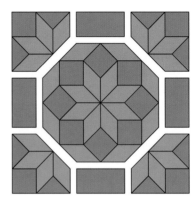

Partial assembly

6. Insert 4 setting rectangles to fill in the edges of the quilt. Each inset has 2 pivot points.

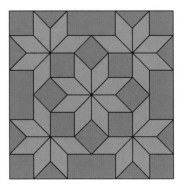

Rolling Star

Finishing

ot every Pineapple Star quilt needs a border. But should you decide to add one, this chapter can help you with the technical issues of measuring and piecing so that your border looks as neat and professional as your Diamond Pineapple blocks. We'll also look at different ways to approach the quilting.

BORDERS

Accurate measurements are key to a border that lies flat. Press the quilt top and lay it out on a flat surface. Ignore any wobblies, or rippling, at the quilt edges, which can skew the results. Measure through the middle of the quilt in both directions to obtain the official length and width (and it's okay if the two measurements are different). Jot down your figures, and keep them and a calculator handy.

CLASSIC BORDER

This border, described on page 23, is made by sewing strips to the quilt top. Sew on the side inner border strips first and then the top and bottom inner border strips, pressing as you go. Repeat this piecing and pressing sequence for the outer border strips. Multiple-strip borders can be made the same way. If you remeasure the quilt after each addition, you'll be able to cut each new pair of strips to the precise length.

Press in any direction that makes sense for the quilt. Generally, I press toward the outer edge of

the quilt. But if I am planning a quilting design that will meander across the border strips, I press the seams open.

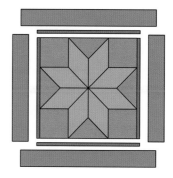

Classic border assembly

BORDERS WITH CORNERSTONES

This border, described on page 24, is also easy to piece. Sew the inner and outer border strips together, to make four border units. Sew the side borders to the quilt top. Press toward the borders. Sew a cornerstone block to both ends of each remaining pieced border. Press the seam allowance toward the borders. Join the cornerstone border units to the top and bottom edges of the quilt top. Press as desired.

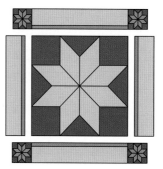

Cornerstone border assembly

FLOATING LeMOYNE STARS

This floating star border treatment, described on page 24, takes time to calculate, but the result is worth it. In this example, the center star measures about 45⅜" x 45⅜". The LeMoyne Star blocks in the border measure 8½" x 8½". Here's how to calculate the dimensions for the spacer strips and the inner border to make everything come out right. You can use this method for any size star and border block; just plug in your own numbers.

1. Add quilt measurement + block measurement + block measurement.

$$45⅜" + 8½" + 8½" = 62⅜"$$

2. Divide the Step 1 result by the block measurement. Round down to the nearest whole number. This is the number of blocks on each outside edge of the quilt. The spacer count is 1 less than the block count.

$$62⅜" ÷ 8½" = 7.338, \text{ rounds down}$$
$$\text{to 7 blocks per edge}$$

There are 6 spacers per edge.

3. Select a finished spacer width that you think would look good in the border. Multiply this number by the spacer count. Multiply the block width by the block count. Add the two results together.

1" sample spacer width
1" x 6 spacers = 6"
8½" x 7 blocks = 59½"
6" + 59½" = 65½"

4. Subtract the Step 1 result from the Step 3 result. Divide by 2 to determine the inner border width. If the Step 1 result is the same as or larger than the Step 3 result, pick a wider spacer width and try again.

$$65½" − 62⅜" = 3⅛"$$
$$3⅛" ÷ 2 = 1⁹⁄₁₆", \text{ inner border width}$$

5. Jot down the spacer finished width (the length is the same as the block size). Add ½" for the seam allowance to determine the cut size. Multiply the spacer count by 4 sides to determine the number of spacers to cut and the number of blocks to make.

Spacer finished size: 1" x 8½"
Spacer cut size: 1½" x 9"
6 spacers per side x 4 sides = 24 spacers,
24 blocks

Once you've completed these calculations, measure through the middle of the quilt to determine the correct length for borders. Cut the inner borders and spacer strips. Piece the star blocks. Lay out all your pieces; your block count and proportions may be different from the assembly diagram. Sew the top and bottom inner borders to the quilt top, measuring through the middle of the quilt to determine the correct length. Press. Repeat to add the side inner borders. Join the star blocks and spacer strips into four borders, as shown. Join the top and bottom star borders to the quilt top. Press. Add the side borders. Press.

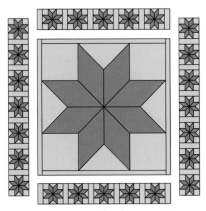

LeMoyne Stars border assembly

QUILTING

The drama and complexity of the Pineapple Star quilt, not to mention the effort you've just put into making the top, calls for good quilting, either by hand or machine. The large setting squares and triangles are prime spaces to showcase your needlework skills, particularly if a plain or subtle fabric is used. Think outside the quilting box, to techniques like trapunto and appliqué. If a busy, patterned fabric is used for the setting blocks, make your quilting design less fancy. Lines or grids work well in these instances. The border needs your quilting attention, too. If you go heavy in the center of the quilt and skimp in the border, the edge of the quilt will wobble. And even though the Diamond Pineapple blocks are made of patterned fabrics, interesting design elements can be quilted into them as well.

There are three quilting design approaches I like to consider:

- ◆ Accenting angles ◆ Adding curves
- ◆ Quilting intricate details

I used my virtual quilt software to test-drive all three on my quilt *Younger Than Springtime,* on page 58. Let me show you.

In the straight-line quilting school, we accent the angles and stitch at the base of individual strips, either in-the-ditch or ¼" inside the seam. Similar motifs can be carried over into the setting blocks and border. You can quilt designs like LeMoyne Stars or diamonds, even if you didn't piece them.

Straight line virtual quilting

Straight line real quilting

Curved quilting lines are a personal favorite. They tone down the angularity and seem to balance out the linear nature of the piecing. Designs based on circles soften the quilt and are also easy to stitch. If you use curves in the center of the quilt, keep the theme rolling and put curves in the border, too.

Curved line virtual quilting

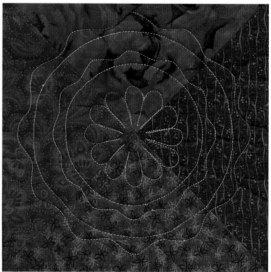

Curved line real quilting

Intricate virtual quilting

Intricate quilting lets you pull out all the stops. Look for design motifs like curlicues, flowers, or hearts in your fabrics, and translate them into quilting or trapunto. Just because a Diamond Pineapple block has patterned fabric doesn't mean you can't lay an intricate quilting design over it. If hand quilting isn't your forte, go for free-motion machine quilting. Try a single design over the whole block. Take designs meant for small LeMoyne Star diamonds and blow them up to fill a large Diamond Pineapple block. Intricate quilting over the patterned block won't always show up from a distance, but it's a delightful surprise for those who come up close!

Intricate real quilting

PROJECTS

Τhis section contains nine Pineapple Star projects. The first is a classic Star of Bethlehem variation. The quilt projects that follow become progressively more sophisticated in the use of fabrics, settings, and border. You'll no doubt be tempted to mix and match these various elements to come up with your own designs.

DIAMOND PINEAPPLE BLOCKS

As I've discussed earlier, each Diamond Pineapple block can be made in either four or five rounds and in three different sizes—large, medium, and miniature—for six different size options in all.

Once you choose a block size, follow the fabric guide to select the fabrics you'll need for your quilt. Because I know you like the flexibility to choose a different fabric for the border, border yardages are listed separately.

BLOCK PATTERNS TO PHOTOCOPY ARE ON THE PATTERN INSERT; TO ORDER PREPRINTED NEWSPRINT PATTERNS, SEE PAGE 95.

Refer to the appropriate block cutting guide to cut the fabric you will need for piecing on a paper foundation. Each guide lists the requirements for one block; the project directions tell you how many blocks to make for the quilt. Here's a sample cutting chart with annotations to help you get started.

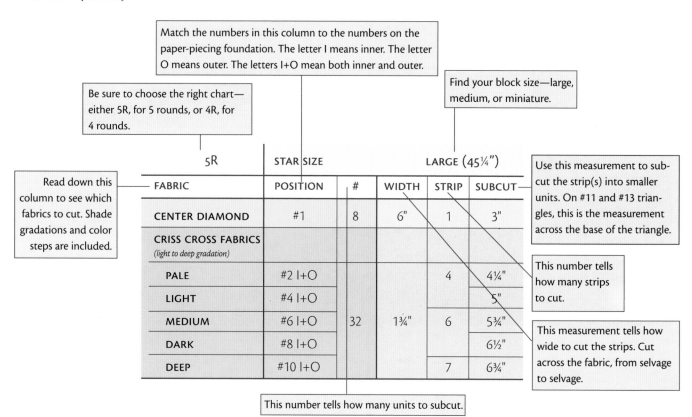

Match the numbers in this column to the numbers on the paper-piecing foundation. The letter I means inner. The letter O means outer. The letters I+O mean both inner and outer.

Be sure to choose the right chart—either 5R, for 5 rounds, or 4R, for 4 rounds.

Find your block size—large, medium, or miniature.

Read down this column to see which fabrics to cut. Shade gradations and color steps are included.

Use this measurement to sub-cut the strip(s) into smaller units. On #11 and #13 triangles, this is the measurement across the base of the triangle.

This number tells how many strips to cut.

This measurement tells how wide to cut the strips. Cut across the fabric, from selvage to selvage.

This number tells how many units to subcut.

5R — **STAR SIZE** — **LARGE (45¼")**

FABRIC	POSITION	#	WIDTH	STRIP	SUBCUT
CENTER DIAMOND	#1	8	6"	1	3"
CRISS CROSS FABRICS *(light to deep gradation)*					
PALE	#2 I+O			4	4¼"
LIGHT	#4 I+O				5"
MEDIUM	#6 I+O	32	1¾"	6	5¾"
DARK	#8 I+O				6½"
DEEP	#10 I+O			7	6¾"

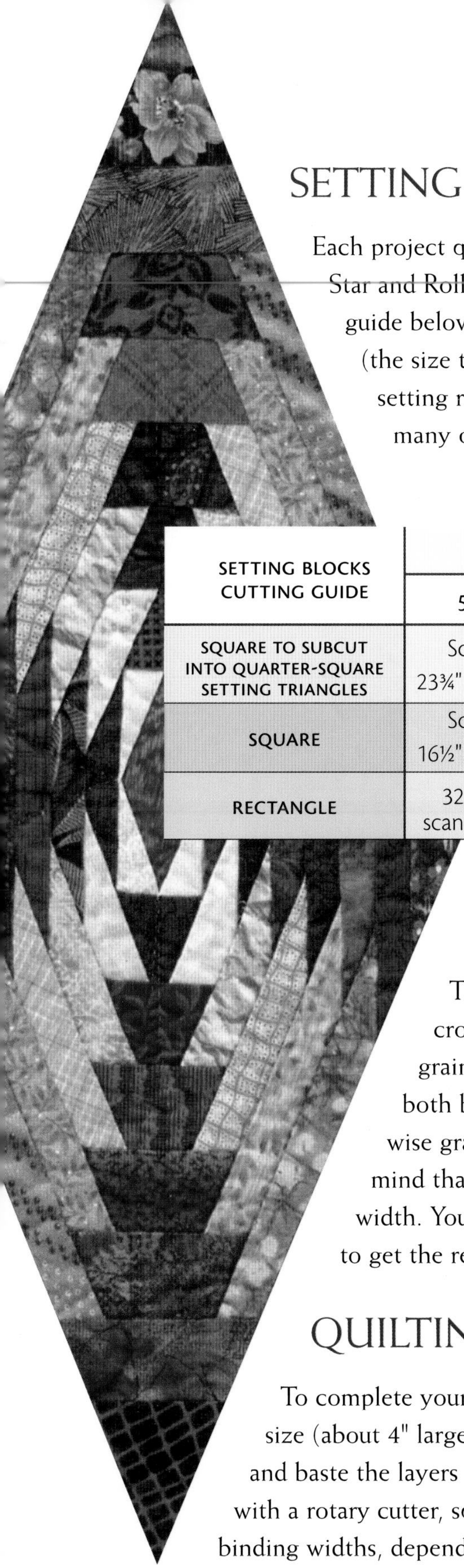

SETTING BLOCKS

Each project quilt uses a combination of setting squares and setting triangles. Broken Star and Rolling Star settings require setting rectangles as well. Follow the cutting guide below to cut the setting blocks for your project. Cut the larger-size square first (the size that will be subcut into triangles) and then cut the setting squares and any setting rectangles from the remaining fabric. The project directions specify how many of each type are needed.

SETTING BLOCKS CUTTING GUIDE	LARGE		MEDIUM		MINIATURE	
	5R	4R	5R	4R	5R	4R
SQUARE TO SUBCUT INTO QUARTER-SQUARE SETTING TRIANGLES	Scant 23¾" x 23¾"	Generous 20" x 20"	13¼" x 13¼"	11¼" x 11¼"	7¼" x 7¼"	6¼" x 6¼"
SQUARE	Scant 16½" x 16½"	Generous 13¾" x 13¾"	9" x 9"	Generous 7½" x 7½"	4¾" x 4¾"	Generous 4" x 4"
RECTANGLE	32⅜" x scant 16½"	27⅛" x generous 13¾"	17½" x 9"	14⅝" x generous 7½"	9" x 4¾"	7⅝" x generous 4"

BORDER

The yardage in the fabric guides assumes border strips will be cut on the crosswise grain, from selvage to selvage. To cut borders on the lengthwise grain, you may need to allow extra yardage. When a single fabric is used for both borders and blocks, you may wish to cut the border strips on the lengthwise grain first and then cut the remaining fabric into strips for piecing. Keep in mind that these crosswise strips will be shorter than the standard 40" useable width. You will need to cut more of them than the number indicated on the chart to get the required number of subcut units.

QUILTING AND FINISHING

To complete your quilt, you will need batting and a backing fabric cut to the appropriate size (about 4" larger than the finished quilt size). Layer the quilt top, batting, and backing, and baste the layers together. Quilt by hand or machine. Trim the excess batting and backing with a rotary cutter, squaring up the quilt in the process. Bind the edges. I use several finished binding widths, depending on the scale of the quilt: LARGE: ⅜" WIDE

MEDIUM: ¼" WIDE

MINIATURE: ³/₁₆" WIDE

Younger than Springtime

SHARON REXROAD, 2003
Quilted by Linda Huff.

STYLE: Star of Bethlehem

DESIGN FEATURES: Classic Pineapple Star

EDGE: Classic two-strip border

BLOCKS: 8 Diamond Pineapples, 4 setting squares, 4 setting triangles

FINISHED SIZES	LARGE		MEDIUM		MINIATURE	
	5R	4R (shown)	5R	4R	5R	4R
QUILT (includes binding)	67½" x 67½"	58½" x 58½"	36½" x 36½"	31⅝ x 31⅝"	18½" x 18½"	16" x 16"
PINEAPPLE STAR	54¼"	45¼"	29"	24⅛"	14½"	12"

FABRIC		LARGE		MEDIUM		MINIATURE	
		5R	4R (shown)	5R	4R	5R	4R
CENTER DIAMOND	CORAL CHECK	¼ yd		⅛ yd		⅛ yd	
CRISSCROSS	CREAM	1½ yds	1⅛ yds	¾ yd	⅝ yd	⅜ yd	
FOCUS (excludes border & binding)	FLORAL	1½ yds	1¼ yds	⅞ yd	½ yd	⅜ yd	
RING (excludes inner border)	GOLD	1¼ yds	1 yd	⅝ yd	½ yd	⅜ yd	
SETTING BLOCKS	ROSE	1¾ yds	1½ yds	¾ yd			¼ yd
INNER BORDER (may add to ring fabric)	GOLD	⅜ yd		¼ yd		⅛ yd	
OUTER BORDER (may add to focus fabric)	FLORAL	1½ yds		½ yd		¼ yd	
BINDING (may add to focus fabric)		⅝ yd		¼ yd		⅛ yd	

CUTTING GUIDES

Refer to the guides below and on page 60 to cut the appropriate border, block pieces, and binding for your size quilt. If you prefer, the border strips can be cut on the lengthwise grain; you will need more yardage. Refer to the guide on page 57 to cut the setting blocks.

BORDER/BINDING CUTTING GUIDE	LARGE		MEDIUM		MINIATURE	
	5R	4R (shown)	5R	4R	5R	4R
INNER BORDER	8 strips 1⅜"	8 strips 1⅜"	4 strips 1"	4 strips 1"	2 strips ¾"	2 strips ¾"
OUTER BORDER	8 strips 6"	8 strips 6"	4 strips 3½"	4 strips 3½"	2 strips 2"	2 strips 2"
BINDING	7 strips 2⅜"	7 strips 2⅜"	4 strips 1⅝"	4 strips 1⅝"	2 strips 1¼"	2 strips 1¼"

ASSEMBLY

1. Paper piece 8 Diamond Pineapple blocks. (See Piecing the Block, pages 27–35.)

2. Join the blocks in a Star of Bethlehem. (See Piecing the Star, pages 38–43.)

3. Insert 4 setting triangles and 4 setting squares. (See Setting Blocks, pages 45–48.) If the setting block fabric has a directional pattern, be consistent in its placement. View the fabric from a distance; up close, a directional pattern may not be evident.

4. Add the inner and outer borders to the quilt top. (See Classic Border, page 51.)

5. Layer and finish the quilt. (See Quilting, page 53–55). This project quilt has intricate quilting on top of the star blocks and setting blocks.

4R

FABRIC	POSITION	#	LARGE (45¼")			MEDIUM (24⅛")			MINIATURE (12")		
			WIDTH	STRIP	SUBCUT	WIDTH	STRIP	SUBCUT	WIDTH	STRIP	SUBCUT
CENTER DIAMOND	#1	8	6"	1	3"	3⅜"	1	1¾"	2"	1	1¼"
CRISSCROSS	#2 I+O			4	4¼"		2	2½"			1½"
	#4 I+O	32	1¾"		5"	1¼"	3	3"	1"	2	1¾"
	#6 I+O			6	5¾"			3½"			2"
	#8 I+O				6½"		4	4"			2¼"
FOCUS FABRIC	#3 S			2	3"		1	1¾"			1¼"
	#5 S		1¾"		4¼"	1¼"		2½"	1"	1	1½"
	#7 S	16		3	5½"		2	3⅛"			2"
	#9 S				6¾"			3¾"			2¼"
	#11 Triangle		8"	2	6⅝"	5"	1	4⅛"	3⅛"	1	2⅝"
RING FABRIC	#3 L			3	6¼"			4¼"			2"
	#5 L				6¾"			4½"		1	2¼"
	#7 L	16	1¾"	4	7¼"	1¼"	2	4¾"	1"		2⅜"
	#9 L				7¾"			5"		2	3"
	#11 L			2*	3½"			2¾"		1*	2"

Ample leftovers from previous strips to cut these subcut pieces.

5R

FABRIC	POSITION	#	LARGE (54¼")			MEDIUM (29")			MINIATURE (14½")		
			WIDTH	STRIP	SUBCUT	WIDTH	STRIP	SUBCUT	WIDTH	STRIP	SUBCUT
CENTER DIAMOND	#1	8	6"	1	3"	3⅜"	1	1¾"	2"	1	1¼"
CRISSCROSS	#2 I+O			4	4¼"		2	2½"			1½"
	#4 I+O				5"		3	3"			1¾"
	#6 I+O	32	1¾"	6	5¾"	1¼"		3½"	1"	2	2"
	#8 I+O				6½"		4	4"			2¼"
	#10 I+O			7	7¾"			4½"			2½"
FOCUS FABRIC	#3 S			2	3"		1	1¾"			1¼"
	#5 S				4¼"			2½"			1½"
	#7 S	16	1¾"	3	5½"	1¼"	2	3⅛"	1"	1	2"
	#9 S				6¾"			3¾"			2¼"
	#11 S			4	8¼"			4⅝"			2½"
	#13 Triangle		9½"	2	7⅞"	5⅞"	2	4⅞"	3½"	1	2⅞"
RING FABRIC	#3 L			3	6¼"			4¼"			2"
	#5 L				6¾"		2	4½"		1	2¼"
	#7 L	16	1¾"	4	7¼"	1¼"		4¾"	1"		2⅜"
	#9 L				7¾"			5"			2½"
	#11 L				8¼"		3	5¼"		2	3"
	#13 L			2*	3½"		2*	2¾"		1*	2"

Use leftovers from previous strips.

Springtime Glow

SHARON REXROAD, 2004

STYLE: Star of Bethlehem

DESIGN FEATURES: Luminosity
(light to dark gradation), fussy-cut tips

EDGE: Cornerstone border with Lily blocks

BLOCKS: 8 Diamond Pineapple, 4 Lily Cornerstones,
4 setting squares, 4 setting triangles

FINISHED SIZES	LARGE		MEDIUM		MINIATURE	
	5R	4R	5R	4R (shown)	5R	4R
QUILT (includes binding)	66¾" x 66¾"	57¾" x 57¾"	36¾" x 36¾"	31⅞" X 31⅞"	18" x 18"	15½" x 15½"
PINEAPPLE STAR	54¼"	45¼"	29"	24⅛"	14½"	12"
LILY BLOCK	6" x 6"	6" x 6"	3⅝" x 3⅝"	3⅝" x 3⅝"	1½" x ½"	1½" x ½"

FABRIC		LARGE		MEDIUM		MINIATURE	
		5R	4R	5R	4R (shown)	5R	4R
CENTER DIAMOND (includes lily diamonds)	NAVY PRINT	⅜ yd		¼ yd		⅛ yd	
CRISSCROSS (gradation)							
PALE	PALE GREEN	¼ yd		⅛ yd			
LIGHT	LIGHT GREEN			¼ yd			
MEDIUM	MEDIUM GREEN	⅜ yd				⅛ yd	
DARK (includes lily triangles)	DARK GREEN	½ yd		⅜ yd			
DEEP	DEEP GREEN	½ yd	not used	¼ yd	not used	⅛ yd	not used
FOCUS (excludes border, inc. lily pieces)	FLORAL	1½ yds	1¼ yds	¾ yd	⅝ yd	⅜ yd	
RING (excludes binding)	PURPLE PLAID	1⅛ yds	1 yd	⅝ yd	½ yd	⅜ yd	
SETTING BLOCKS	MAGENTA	1¾ yds	1½ yds	¾ yd		¼ yd	
BORDER (may add to focus fabric)*	FLORAL	1⅝ yds	1⅜ yds	⅞ yd	¾ yd	½ yd	
BINDING (may add to ring fabric)	PURPLE PLAID	⅝ yd	½ yd	¼ yd		⅛ yd	

Yardage allows for borders to be cut lengthwise.

Cutting Guides

Refer to the following guides to cut the appropriate border, binding, Diamond Pineapple, and Lily block pieces for your size quilt. If you prefer, the border strips can be cut on the lengthwise grain. (See Borders on page 57 for more details). Refer to the guide on page 57 to cut the setting blocks.

BORDER/BINDING CUTTING GUIDE	LARGE		MEDIUM		MINIATURE	
	5R	4R	5R	4R (shown)	5R	4R
BORDER (choose one cut only)						
CROSSWISE CUT	7 strips 6½"	6 strips 6½"	4 strips 4⅛"	4 strips 4⅛"	2 strips 2"	2 strips 2"
LENGTHWISE CUT (generous)	4 strips 6½" x 56"	4 strips 6½" x 47"	4 strips 4⅛" x 31"	4 strips 4⅛" x 26"	4 strips 2" x 16½"	4 strips 2" x 14"
BINDING	8 strips 2⅜"	7 strips 2⅜"	4 strips 1⅝"	4 strips 1⅝"	2 strips 1¼"	2 strips 1¼"

4R

4R FABRIC	STAR SIZE POSITION	#	LARGE (45¼") WIDTH	STRIP	SUBCUT	MEDIUM (24⅛") WIDTH	STRIP	SUBCUT	MINIATURE (12") WIDTH	STRIP	SUBCUT
CENTER DIAMOND	#1	8	6"	1	3"	3⅜"	1	1¾"	2"	1	1¼"
CRISSCROSS FABRICS (light to dark gradation)											
PALE	#2 I+O			4	4¼"		2	2½"			1½"
LIGHT	#4 I+O	32	1¾"		5"	1¼"	3	3"	1"	2	1¾"
MEDIUM	#6 I+O			6	5¾"			3½"			2"
DARK	#8 I+O				6½"		4	4"			2¼"
FOCUS FABRIC	#3 S			2	3"		1	1¾"			1¼"
	#5 S		1¾"		4¼"	1¼"		2½"	1"	1	1½"
	#7 S	16		3	5½"		2	3⅛"			2"
	#9 S				6¾"			3¾"			2¼"
FUSSY CUT	#11 Triangle		8"	2	6⅝"	5"	1	4⅛"	3⅛"	1	2⅝"
RING FABRIC	#3 L			3	6¼"			4¼"			2"
	#5 L				6¾"			4½"		1	2¼"
	#7 L	16	1¾"	4	7¼"	1¼"	2	4¾"	1"		2⅜"
	#9 L				7¾"			5"		2	3"
	#11 L			2	3½"			2¾"		1	2"

5R

5R FABRIC	STAR SIZE POSITION	#	LARGE (54¼") WIDTH	STRIP	SUBCUT	MEDIUM (29") WIDTH	STRIP	SUBCUT	MINIATURE (14½") WIDTH	STRIP	SUBCUT
CENTER DIAMOND	#1	8	6"	1	3"	3⅜"	1	1¾"	2"	1	1¼"
CRISSCROSS FABRICS (light to deep gradation)											
PALE	#2 I+O			4	4¼"		2	2½"			1½"
LIGHT	#4 I+O				5"		3	3"			1¾"
MEDIUM	#6 I+O	32	1¾"	6	5¾"	1¼"		3½"	1"	2	2"
DARK	#8 I+O				6½"		4	4"			2¼"
DEEP	#10 I+O			7	7¾"			4½"			2½"
FOCUS FABRIC	#3 S			2	3"		1	1¾"			1¼"
	#5 S				4¼"			2½"			1½"
	#7 S	16	1¾"	3	5½"	1¼"	2	3⅛"	1"	1	2"
	#9 S				6¾"			3¾"			2¼"
	#11 S			4	8¼"			4⅝"			2½"
FUSSY CUT	#13 Triangle		9½"	2	7⅞"	5⅞"	2	4⅞"	3½"	1	2⅞"
RING FABRIC	#3 L			3	6¼"			4¼"			2"
	#5 L				6¾"		2	4½"		1	2¼"
	#7 L	16	1¾"	4	7¼"	1¼"		4¾"	1"		2⅜"
	#9 L				7¾"			5"			2½"
	#11 L				8¼"		3	5¼"		2	3"
	#13 L			2	3½"		2	2¾"		1	2"

LILY BLOCKS (4) CUTTING GUIDE		LARGE		MEDIUM		MINIATURE	
		5R	4R	5R	4R *(shown)*	5R	4R *(shown)*
FABRIC	POSITION						
CENTER DIAMOND	A	Cut 2 strips, 2¼". Subcut diagonally every 2¼" to make 16 diamonds.		Cut 1 strip, 1⅝". Subcut diagonally every 1⅝" to make 16 diamonds.		Cut 1 scant 1" strip. Subcut diagonally every scant 1" to make 16 diamonds.	
DARK CRISSCROSS	B	Cut 2 squares 4⅜" x 4⅜". Subcut diagonally in half to make 4 triangles.		Cut 2 squares 3" x 3". Subcut diagonally in half to make 4 triangles.		Cut 2 squares 1¾" x 1¾". Subcut diagonally in half to make 4 triangles.	
FOCUS	C	Cut 4 squares 3" x 3".		Cut 4 squares 2" x 2".		Cut 4 squares 1⅛" x 1⅛".	
FOCUS	D	Cut 2 squares 4¾" x 4¾". Subcut diagonally in both directions to make 8 triangles.		Cut 2 squares 3⅜" x 3⅜". Subcut diagonally in both directions to make 8 triangles.		Cut 2 squares 2⅛" x 2⅛". Subcut diagonally in both directions to make 8 triangles.	

ASSEMBLY

1. Paper-piece 8 Diamond Pineapple blocks. (See Piecing the Block, pages 27–35.)

2. Join the blocks in a Star of Bethlehem. (See Piecing the Star, pages 38–43.)

3. Insert 4 setting squares and 4 setting triangles. (See Setting Blocks, pages 45–48.)

4. Piece 4 A diamonds together to make a half-star. Sew triangle B to the long edge. Set in 1 C and 2 D. Make 4 Lily blocks.

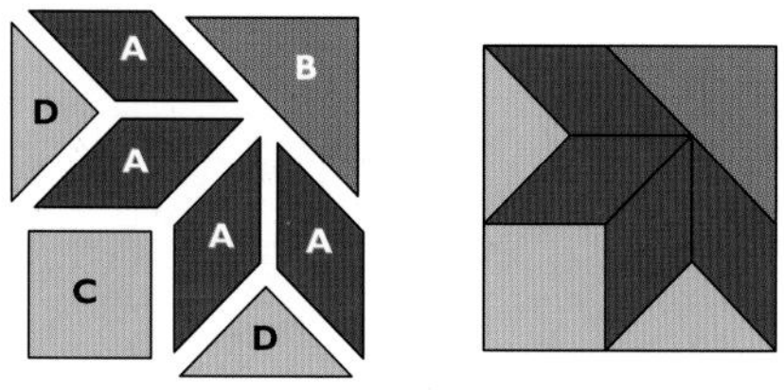

5. Add the borders and Lily blocks to the quilt top. (See Borders with Cornerstones, page 51.) Orient the Lily blocks as shown in the quilt photo.

6. Layer and finish the quilt. (See Quilting, pages 53–55.) This project quilt has straight line quilting in the blocks and border and intricate quilting in the setting blocks.

Lily block
Make 4.

Oriental
Diamond
Delight

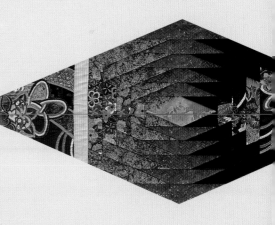

JANICE LIPPINCOTT, 2002

STYLE: Star of Bethlehem, floating setting

DESIGN FEATURES: Interior glow, interior zinger, strips companion print combo, fussy-cut tips

EDGE: Piped binding

BLOCKS: 8 Diamond Pineapple, 4 setting squares (elongated), 4 setting triangles (elongated)

FINISHED SIZES	LARGE		MEDIUM		MINIATURE	
	5R *(shown)*	4R	5R	4R	5R	4R
QUILT *(includes binding)*	59" x 59"	49¼" x 49¼"	31½" x 31½"	26½" x 26½"	17½" x 17½"	13¾" x 13¾"
PINEAPPLE STAR	54¼"	45¼"	29"	24⅛"	14½"	12"

FABRIC		LARGE		MEDIUM		MINIATURE	
		5R *(shown)*	4R	5R	4R	5R	4R
CENTER DIAMOND	POPPY BATIK	¼ yd		⅛ yd		⅛ yd	
CRISSCROSS							
LIGHT	SOFT GREEN	¾ yd	⅝ yd	⅜ yd		¼ yd	
DARK	RICH GREEN	¾ yd	⅝ yd	⅜ yd		¼ yd	
FOCUS *(add more for fussy cuts)*	JUMBO FLORAL	1 yd	⅞ yd	not used		not used	
	LARGE FLORAL	not used		⅔ yd	½ yd	⅜ yd	¼ yd
COMPANION	LARGE FLORAL	⅜ yd		not used		not used	
	MEDIUM FLORAL	not used		¼ yd		⅛ yd*	
ZINGER	GOLD	⅛ yd		⅛ yd		⅛ yd	
RING *(excludes piping)*	BURGUNDY	1⅛ yds	⅞ yd	⅝ yd	½ yd	¼ yd	
SETTING BLOCKS	TAUPE	1⅞ yds	1⅜ yds	¾ yd		¼ yd	
PIPING *(may add to ring fabric)*	BURGUNDY	¼ yd		⅛ yd		⅛ yd	
BINDING *(may add to Setting Block fabric)*	TAUPE	⅝ yd (7 strips 2⅜")	½ yd (6 strips 2⅜")	¼ yd (4 strips 1⅝")	¼ yd (3 strips 1⅝")	⅛ yd (2 strips 1¼")	

* Only ½ strip is needed per subcut.

CUTTING GUIDES

Refer to the guides below and on pages 67 and 68 to cut the appropriate Diamond Pineapple pieces and setting blocks for your size quilt. The setting blocks in this quilt are enlarged so that the star visually floats against the background. Cut the larger-size square first (the size that will be subcut into triangles) and then cut the corner squares from the remaining fabric.

SETTING BLOCKS CUTTING GUIDE	LARGE		MEDIUM		MINIATURE	
	5R *(shown)*	4R	5R	4R	5R	4R
SQUARE TO SUBCUT INTO QUARTER-SQUARE SETTING TRIANGLES	27⅞" x 27⅞"	23¾" x 23¾"	15½" x 15½"	13¼" x 13¼"	8⅜" x 8⅜"	7¼" x 7¼"
SETTING SQUARES	18½" x 18½"	15½" x 15½"	10" x 10"	8½" x 8½"	6" x 6"	4⅝" x 4⅝"
TRIANGLE TRIM *(see Assembly Step 3)*	2⅜"	2⅛"	1⅜"	1¼"	⅞"	13/16"

4R	STAR SIZE		LARGE (45¼")			MEDIUM (24⅛")			MINIATURE (12")		
FABRIC	POSITION	#	WIDTH	STRIP	SUBCUT	WIDTH	STRIP	SUBCUT	WIDTH	STRIP	SUBCUT
CENTER DIAMOND	#1	8	6"	1	3"	3⅜"	1	1¾"	2"	1	1¼"
INNER CRISSCROSS *(lighter color)*	#2 I			2	4¼"		1	2½"			1½"
	#4 I	16	1¾"		5"			3"	1"	1	1¾"
	#6 I			3	5¾"	1¼"	2	3½"			2"
	#8 I				6½"			4"			2¼"
OUTER CRISSCROSS *(darker color)*	#2 O			2	4¼"		1	2½"			1½"
	#4 O	16	1¾"		5"	1¼"		3"	1"	1	1¾"
	#6 O			3	5¾"		2	3½"			2"
	#8 O				6½"			4"			2¼"
FOCUS FABRIC *(Outer plus both Triangles)*	#3 S (O)			1	3"			1¾"			1¼"
	#5 S (O)	8	1¾"		4¼"	1¼"	1	2½"	1"	1	1½"
	#7 S (O)			2	5½"			3⅛"			2"
	#9 S (O)				6¾"			3¾"			2¼"
FUSSY CUT	#11 Triangle	16	8"	3	6⅝"	5"	1	4⅛"	3⅛"	1	2⅝"
COMPANION FABRIC *(Inner)*	#3 S (I)			1	3"			1¾"			1¼"
	#5 S (I)	8	1¾"		4¼"	1¼"	1	2½"	1"	½	1½"
	#7 S (I)			2	5½"			3⅛"			2"
ZINGER	#9 S (I)	8	1¾"	2	6¾"	1¼"	1	3¾"	1"	1	2¼"
RING FABRIC	#3 L			3	6¼"			4¼"			2"
	#5 L				6¾"			4½"		1	2¼"
	#7 L	16	1¾"	4	7¼"	1¼"	2	4¾"	1"		2⅜"
	#9 L				7¾"			5"		2	3"
	#11 L			2	3½"			2¾"		1	2"

Assembly

1. Paper-piece 8 Diamond Pineapple blocks. (See Piecing the Block, pages 27–35.)

2. Join the blocks in a Star of Bethlehem. (See Piecing the Star, pages 38–43.)

3. Measure from the tip along the triangle's long side, using the appropriate measurement for your size quilt (see the Setting Blocks Cutting Guide). Trim each triangle setting block as shown.

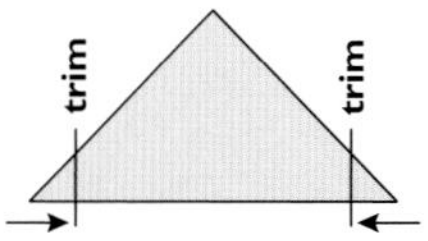

Trim triangle setting block.

4. Insert 4 setting triangles and 4 setting squares. (See Setting Blocks, pages 45–48.) The trimmed edges of the triangles extend the straight edge of the Diamond Pineapple blocks to create the floating star.

5. Layer and finish the quilt. (See Quilting, pages 53–55.) The project quilt has straight lines of quilting in the Diamond Pineapple blocks and radiating lines of quilting in the setting blocks.

6. From piping fabric, cut ¾"-wide strips. Piece strips as needed to make one continuous strip for each side of your quilt. Press each strip in half, right side out. Baste a piping strip to each edge, then secure it in the binding seam.

5R	STAR SIZE	#	LARGE (54¼")			MEDIUM (29")			MINIATURE (14½")		
FABRIC	POSITION	#	WIDTH	STRIP	SUBCUT	WIDTH	STRIP	SUBCUT	WIDTH	STRIP	SUBCUT
CENTER DIAMOND	#1	8	6"	1	3"	3⅜"	1	1¾"	2"	1	1¼"
INNER CRISSCROSS (lighter color)22	#2 I			2	4¼"		1	2½"			1½"
	#4 I				5"			3"			1¾"
	#6 I	16	1¾"	3	5¾"	1¼"		3½"	1"	1	2"
	#8 I				6½"		2	4"			2¼"
	#10 I			4	7¾"			4½"			2½"
OUTER CRISSCROSS (darker color)	#2 O			2	4¼"		1	2½"			1½"
	#4 O				5"			3"			1¾"
	#6 O	16	1¾"	3	5¾"	1¼"	2	3½"	1"	1	2"
	#8 O				6½"			4"			2¼"
	#10 O			4	7¾"			4½"			2½"
FOCUS FABRIC (Outer plus both Triangles)	#3 S (O)			1	3"			1¾"			1¼"
	#5 S (O)				4¼"			2½"			1½"
	#7 S (O)	8	1¾"		5½"	1¼"	1	3⅛"	1"	1	2"
	#9 S (O)			2	6¾"			3¾"			2¼"
	#11 S (O)				8¼"			4⅝"			2½"
FUSSY CUT	#13 Triangle	16	9½"	2	7⅞"	5⅞"	2	4⅞"	3½"	1	2⅞"
COMPANION FABRIC (Inner)	#3 S (I)			1	3"			1¾"			1¼"
	#5 S (I)	8	1¾"		4¼"	1¼"	1	2½"	1"	½	1½"
	#7 S (I)			2	5½"			3⅛"			2"
	#9 S (I)				6¾"			3¾"			2¼"
ZINGER	#11 S (I)	8	1¾"	2	8¼"	1¼"	1	4⅝"	1"	1	2½"
RING FABRIC	#3 L			3	6¼"			4¼"			2"
	#5 L				6¾"		2	4½"		1	2¼"
	#7 L	16	1¾"		7¼"	1¼"		4¾"	1"		2⅜"
	#9 L			4	7¾"			5"			2½"
	#11 L				8¼"		3	5¼"		2	3"
	#13 L			2	3½"		2	2¾"		1	2"

Ribbons & Lace

Sharon Rexroad, 2004
Quilted by Linda Huff.

Style: Star of Bethlehem

Design Features: Double LeMoyne Star center, interior glow, lace doily embellishment

Edge: Lace inserted before binding

Blocks: 8 Diamond Pineapples, 4 setting squares, 4 setting triangles

FINISHED SIZES	LARGE		MEDIUM		MINIATURE	
	5R	4R (shown)	5R	4R	5R	4R
QUILT (includes binding)	55" x 55"	46" x 46"	29½" x 29½"	24⅝" x 24⅝"	16⅛" x 16⅛"	13⅝" x 13⅝"

FABRIC		LARGE		MEDIUM		MINIATURE	
		5R	4R (shown)	5R	4R	5R	4R
CENTER DIAMOND	GREEN	¼ yd		⅛ yd		⅛ yd	
CRISSCROSS							
LIGHT	LIGHT TEAL	¾ yd	⅝ yd	½ yd	⅜ yd	¼ yd	
DARK	DARK TEAL						
FOCUS (includes 24 D)	PEACH MARBLE	1¼ yds	⅞ yd	⅝ yd	½ yd	⅜ yd	¼ yd
RING	OLIVE TAN	1 yd		½ yd		¼ yd	
LEMOYNE A	DARK TEAL	¼ yd		⅛ yd		⅛ yd	
LEMOYNE A (add more for fussy cuts)	FLORAL	½ yd		⅛ yd		⅛ yd	
SETTING BLOCKS		1¾ yds	1½ yds	¾ yd		¼ yd	
BINDING (may add to dark crisscross fabric)	DARK TEAL	½ yd 6 strips 2⅜"	⅜ yd 5 strips 2⅜"	¼ yd 4 strips 1⅝"	¼ yd 3 strips 1⅝"	⅛ yd 2 strips 1¼"	
DOILY (need 9)		6" diameter		4" diameter		2" diameter	
LACE EDGING: ½" WIDE FOR LARGE, ⅜" WIDE FOR MEDIUM, ¼" WIDE FOR MINIATURE		6⅝ yds	5⅝ yds	3¾ yds	3¼ yds	2⅛ yds	1⅞ yds

Cutting Guides

Refer to the guides on pages 71 and 72 to cut the appropriate Diamond Pineapple pieces for your size quilt. Refer to the guide on page 57 to cut the setting blocks. Prepare LeMoyne Star templates A and D (see pattern insert), choosing the size appropriate to your quilt. Use template A to cut 8 A diamonds from the dark teal and 16 fussy-cut A diamonds (8 in mirror image) from the floral. Cut 24 D from the peach marble.

4R	STAR SIZE		LARGE (45¼")			MEDIUM (24⅛")			MINIATURE (12")		
FABRIC	POSITION	#	WIDTH	STRIP	SUBCUT	WIDTH	STRIP	SUBCUT	WIDTH	STRIP	SUBCUT
CENTER DIAMOND	#1	8	6"	1	3"	3⅜"	1	1¾"	2"	1	1¼"
INNER CRISSCROSS (lighter color)	#2 I			2	4¼"		1	2½"			1½"
	#4 I	16	1¾"		5"	1¼"		3"	1"	1	1¾"
	#6 I			3	5¾"		2	3½"			2"
	#8 I				6½"			4"			2¼"
OUTER CRISSCROSS (darker color)	#2 O			2	4¼"		1	2½"			1½"
	#4 O	16	1¾"		5"	1¼"		3"	1"	1	1¾"
	#6 O			3	5¾"		2	3½"			2"
	#8 O				6½"			4"			2¼"
FOCUS FABRIC	#3 S			2	3"		1	1¾"			1¼"
	#5 S	16	1¾"		4¼"	1¼"		2½"	1"		1½"
	#7 S			3	5½"		2	3⅛"		1	2"
(Outer only)	#9 S (O)	8		2	6¾"		1	3¾"			2¼"
(Outer only)	#11 Triangle	8	8"	1	6⅝"	5"	1	4⅛"	3⅛"	1	2⅝"
RING FABRIC	#3 L			3	6¼"			4¼"			2"
	#5 L				6¾"			4½"		1	2¼"
	#7 L	16	1¾"	4	7¼"	1¼"	2	4¾"	1"		2⅜"
	#9 L				7¾"			5"		2	3"
	#11 L			2	3½"			2¾"		1	2"

ASSEMBLY

1. Piece 8 Double LeMoyne tips. (See LeMoyne Star Center on page 37.)

2. Layer doily over the right side of the center diamond #1 rectangle. Rotate until scallops extend past both ends of the rectangle and the center of the doily is over the center of the fabric. Use a fabric gluestick to lightly glue the doily to the rectangle. Trim off the doily parts that extend past the edges.

3. Paper-piece 8 Diamond Pineapple blocks. (See Piecing the Block, pages 27–35.) In each five-round block, add a Double LeMoyne tip in the #13-T position. In each four-round block, add a Double LeMoyne tip in the merged #9-S plus #11-T position.

4. Join the blocks together in a Star of Bethlehem. (See Piecing the Star, pages 38–43.) A Double LeMoyne Star will form at the center. Appliqué a crocheted doily to the quilt center.

5. Insert 4 setting triangles and 4 setting squares. (See Setting Blocks, pages 45–48.)

6. Layer and finish the quilt. (See Quilting, pages 53–55.) The project quilt has intricate quilting over the blocks and a diagonal grid quilted across the background.

7. Cut 4 pieces of lace 2" longer than the quilt edges. Baste a lace piece to each edge, scallops toward the quilt center, then secure it in the binding seam.

5R	STAR SIZE		LARGE (54¼")			MEDIUM (29")			MINIATURE (14½")		
FABRIC	POSITION	#	WIDTH	STRIP	SUBCUT	WIDTH	STRIP	SUBCUT	WIDTH	STRIP	SUBCUT
CENTER DIAMOND	#1	8	6"	1	3"	3⅜"	1	1¾"	2"	1	1¼"
INNER CRISSCROSS *(lighter color)*	#2 I			2	4¼"		1	2½"			1½"
	#4 I				5"			3"			1¾"
	#6 I	16	1¾"	3	5¾"	1¼"	2	3½"	1"	1	2"
	#8 I				6½"			4"			2¼"
	#10 I			4	7¾"			4½"			2½"
OUTER CRISSCROSS *(darker color)*1"	#2 O			2	4¼"		1	2½"			1½"
	#4 O	16	1¾"		5"	1¼"		3"	1"	1	1¾"
	#6 O			3	5¾"		2	3½"			2"
	#8 O				6½"			4"			2¼"
	#10 O			4	7¾"			4½"			2½"
FOCUS FABRIC	#3 S			2	3"		1	1¾"			1¼"
	#5 S				4¼"			2½"	1"	1	1½"
	#7 S	16	1¾"	3	5½"	1¼"		3⅛"			2"
	#9 S				6¾"		2	3¾"			2¼"
	#11 S			4	8¼"			4⅝"			2½"
(Outer Only)	#13 Triangle	8	9½"	1	7⅞"	5⅞"	1	4⅞"	3⅞"	1	2⅞"
RING FABRIC	#3 L			3	6¼"			4¼"			2"
	#5 L				6¾"		2	4½"		1	2¼"
	#7 L	16	1¾"	4	7¼"	1¼"		4¾"	1"		2⅜"
	#9 L				7¾"			5"			2½"
	#11 L				8¼"		3	5¼"		2	3"
	#13 L			2	3½"		2	2¾"		1	2"

Butterflies in My Pineapple

KATHY LICHTENDAHL, 2004

STYLE: Star of Bethlehem, floating setting

DESIGN FEATURES: Fussy-cut center diamonds, interior zinger strips, companion print combo

EDGE: Four-strip border with peaks

BLOCKS: 8 Diamond Pineapples, 4 setting squares, 4 setting triangles

FINISHED SIZES	LARGE		MEDIUM		MINIATURE	
	5R	4R (shown)	5R	4R	5R	4R
QUILT (includes binding)	83" x 83"	74" x 74"	43½" x 43½"	38⅝" x 38⅝"	23⅛" x 23⅛"	20⅝" x 20⅝"
PINEAPPLE STAR	54¼"	45¼"	29"	24⅛"	14½"	12"

FABRIC		LARGE		MEDIUM		MINIATURE	
		5R	4R (shown)	5R	4R	5R	4R
CENTER DIAMOND	PINK	¼ yd		¼ yd		⅛ yd	
CRISSCROSS	SOFT GREEN	1½ yds	1⅛ yds	¾ yd	⅝ yd	⅜ yd	
FOCUS (excludes floral borders)	LARGE FLORAL	1⅛ yds	⅞ yd	not used		not used	
	MEDIUM FLORAL	not used		⅝ yd	½ yd	not used	
	SMALL FLORAL	not used		not used		⅜ yd	
ZINGER (excludes border)	OLIVE	¼ yd		⅛ yd		⅛ yd	
COMPANION PRINT (add more for fussy cuts)	JUMBO FLORAL	⅜ yd	¼ yd	not used		not used	
	LARGE FLORAL	not used		¼ yd		not used	
	MEDIUM FLORAL	not used		not used		⅛ yd	
RING (excludes border)	NAVY PRINT	1¼ yds	1 yd	⅝ yd	½ yd	¼ yd	
SETTING BLOCKS (includes extension strips)	PALE MARBLE	2¼ yds	2 yds	⅞ yd	¾ yd	⅜ yd	
FIRST BORDER (may add to ring fabric)	NAVY PRINT	⅝ yd		¼ yd		⅛ yd	
SECOND BORDER (may add to focus fabric)	LARGE FLORAL	⅞ yd		not used		not used	
	MEDIUM FLORAL	not used		⅜ yd			
	SMALL FLORAL	not used		not used		¼ yd	
THIRD BORDER (may add to Zinger fabric)	OLIVE	⅝ yd		¼ yd		⅛ yd	
FOURTH BORDER* (may add to Companion print)	JUMBO FLORAL	2½ yds	2⅛ yds	not used		not used	
	LARGE FLORAL	not used		1⅜ yds	1¼ yds	not used	
	MEDIUM FLORAL	not used		not used		¾ yd	
BINDING	FLORAL	⅔ yd		⅜ yd		¼ yd	

* Yardage allows for borders to be cut lengthwise.

CUTTING GUIDES

Refer to the guides on pages 75 and 76 to cut the appropriate border, binding, and block pieces for your size quilt. Refer to the guide on page 57 to cut the setting blocks. Make border templates A through D (see pattern insert), choosing the size appropriate to your quilt. In this design, the setting block fabric extends into the border area, giving the illusion of a floating star. The unique peaked border helps show off the focus fabric and its larger-scale companion print.

BORDER/BINDING CUTTING GUIDE	LARGE		MEDIUM		MINIATURE	
	5R	4R (shown)	5R	4R	5R	4R
SETTING BLOCK EXTENSION	8 strips 2½" x 28⅝"	8 strips 2½" x 24⅛"	8 strips 1½" x 16"	8 strips 1½" x 13⅝"	8 strips 1" x 8⅝"	8 strips 1" x 7½"
FIRST BORDER	10 strips 1½"	9 strips 1½"	5 strips 1"		3 strips ¾"	
SECOND BORDER	10 strips 2½"	9 strips 2½"	5 strips 1½"		3 strips 1"	
THIRD BORDER	10 strips 1½"	9 strips 1½"	5 strips 1"		3 strips ¾"	
FOURTH BORDER (cut lengthwise)	4 strips 8½" x 84"	4 strips 8½" x 75"	4 strips 4½" x 45"	4 strips 4½" x 40"	4 strips 2½" x 24"	4 strips 2½" x 21"
FOURTH BORDER CORNER	2 squares 7¼" cut once diagonally		2 squares 4¼" cut once diagonally		2 squares 2½" cut once diagonally	
BINDING	9 strips 2⅜"	8 strips 2⅜"	5 strips 1⅝"		3 strips 1¼"	

4R	STAR SIZE		LARGE (45¼")			MEDIUM (24⅛")			MINIATURE (12")		
FABRIC	POSITION	#	WIDTH	STRIP	SUBCUT	WIDTH	STRIP	SUBCUT	WIDTH	STRIP	SUBCUT
CENTER DIAMOND	#1	8	6"	1	3"	3⅜"	1	1¾"	2"	1	1¼"
CRISSCROSS	#2 I+O			4	4¼"		2	2½"			1½"
	#4 I+O	32	1¾"		5"	1¼"	3	3"	1"	2	1¾"
	#6 I+O			6	5¾"			3½"			2"
	#8 I+O				6½"		4	4"			2¼"
FOCUS FABRIC	#3 S	16	1¾"	2	3"	1¼"	1	1¾"	1"	1	1¼"
	#5 S				4¼"			2½"			1½"
	#7 S			3	5½"		2	3⅛"			2"
(Outer Only)	#9 S (O)	8		2	6¾"		1	3¾"			2¼"
(Outer Only)	#11 Triangle		8"	1	6⅝"	5"	1	4⅛"	3⅛"	1	2⅝"
ZINGER (Inner Only)	#9 S (I)	8	1¾"	2	6¾"	1¼"	1	3¾"	1"	1	2¼"
COMPANION PRINT	#11 Triangle	8	8"	1	6⅝"	5"	1	4⅛"	3⅛"	1	2⅝"
RING FABRIC	#3 L			3	6¼"			4¼"			2"
	#5 L				6¾"			4½"		1	2¼"
	#7 L	16	1¾"	4	7¼"	1¼"	2	4¾"	1"		2⅜"
	#9 L				7¾"			5"		2	3"
	#11 L			2*	3½"			2¾"		1*	2"

* Use leftovers from previous strips

ASSEMBLY

1. Paper-piece 8 Diamond Pineapple blocks. (See Piecing the Block, pages 27–35.)

2. Join the blocks in a Star of Bethlehem. (See Piecing the Star, pages 38–43.)

3. Insert 4 setting squares and 4 setting triangles. (See Setting Blocks, pages 45–48.)

4. Sew the first, second, and third border strips together, with the second border in the middle. Press seams open. Make strip sets.

5. Fold 1 strip set from Step 4 in half, right side in. Place template A on top, aligning the seamlines and edges. Cut along the template edges through both layers to make 2 A (1 in mirror image). Do not separate the pieces. Cut 3 more sets of A units from the same strip set. Sew seam AB on each set, stopping and backstitching at B. Press seams open and trim points at top of seam. Cut 4 B from a scrap of Outer Border fabric. Join Bs to As, matching the B and C points. Make 4 AB units. NOTE: Because the pieces become very small, it is challenging to make the middle peak for a quilt using medium-size blocks, and I suggest switching to a classic border for a quilt using miniature blocks.

6. Cut remaining strip sets 1" longer than a Setting Block Extension strip. (For large size, save 4 leftover segments for corner units.) Fold each strip set in half, right side in. Align template C on the unfolded end. Make an angled cut through both layers, even with the edge of the template. Join two strips to each AB unit along the CD edges, backstitching at D.

7. Fold each setting block extension strip in half, right side in. Make a 45° cut at the unfolded end through both layers. Join 2 extension strips to top edge of each border unit, backstitching at D. Realign fabrics to sew extension strips to AB units along AD edges. Press seams open. Sew a border unit to each edge of the quilt top. Press.

8. Cut 4 D from remaining strip set segments. Sew each D to a Fourth Border Corner for triangle. Press. Sew the corner unit onto each corner of the quilt top. Add the fourth border, mitering the corners. Press.

9. Layer and finish the quilt. (See Quilting, pages 53–55.) This project is perfect for beautiful hand quilting.

5R	STAR SIZE		LARGE (54¼")			MEDIUM (29")			MINIATURE (14½")		
FABRIC	POSITION	#	WIDTH	STRIP	SUBCUT	WIDTH	STRIP	SUBCUT	WIDTH	STRIP	SUBCUT
CENTER DIAMOND	#1	8	6"	1	3"	3⅜"	1	1¾"	2"	1	1¼"
CRISSCROSS	#2 I+O				4	4¼"		2	2½"			1½"
	#4 I+O				5"		3	3"			1¾"
	#6 I+O	32	1¾"	6	5¾"	1¼"		3½"	1"	2	2"
	#8 I+O				6½"		4	4"			2¼"
	#10 I+O			7	7¾"			4½"			2½"
FOCUS FABRIC	#3 S			2	3"		1	1¾"			1¼"
	#5 S	16	1¾"		4¼"	1¼"		2½"	1"	1	1½"
	#7 S			3	5½"		2	3⅛"			2"
	#9 S				6¾"			3¾"			2¼"
(Outer Only)	#11 S (O)	8		2	8¼"		1	4⅝"			2½"
(Outer Only)	#13 Triangle	8	9½"	1	7⅞"	5⅞"	1	4⅞"	3½"	1	2⅞"
ZINGER (Inner Only)	#11 S (I)	8	1¾"	2	8¼"	1¼"	1	4⅝"	1"	1	2½"
COMPANION PRINT	#13 Triangle	8	9½"	1	7⅞"	5⅞"	1	4⅞"	3½"	1	2⅞"
RING FABRIC	#3 L			3	6¼"			4¼"			2"
	#5 L				6¾"		2	4½"		1	2¼"
	#7 L	16	1¾"		7¼"	1¼"		4¾"	1"		2⅜"
	#9 L			4	7¾"			5"			2½"
	#11 L				8¼"		3	5¼"		2	3"
	#13 L			2*	3½"		2*	2¾"		1*	2"

Use leftovers from previous strips

Hothouse Flowers

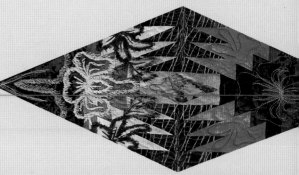

Sharon Rexroad, 2004

Style: Star of Bethlehem

Design Features: Rainbowing, interior Zinger strips

Edge: Pieced border with staggered LeMoyne Star blocks

Blocks: 8 Diamond Pineapples, 28 LeMoyne Stars in four-round quilt, 36 LeMoyne Stars in five-round quilt, 4 setting squares, 4 setting triangles

FABRIC		LARGE		MEDIUM		MINIATURE	
		5R	4R *(shown)*	5R	4R	5R	4R
CENTER DIAMOND	LIME BATIK	¼ yd		¼ yd		⅛ yd	
CRISSCROSS	RAINBOW GRADATION	1½ yds	1⅛ yds	¾ yd	⅝ yd	⅜ yd	
STEP 1	BUTTER YELLOW	¼ yd	not used	⅛ yd	not used	⅛ yd	not used
STEP 2	YELLOW	¼ yd					
STEP 3	YELLOW-ORANGE						
STEP 4	ORANGE						
STEP 5	RED-ORANGE	⅛ yd		⅛ yd		⅛ yd	
STEP 6	RED						
STEP 7	MAGENTA-RED						
STEP 8	RED-MAGENTA	¼ yd					
STEP 9	MAGENTA						
STEP 10	PURPLE-MAGENTA	¼ yd	not used	⅛ yd	not used	⅛ yd	not used
FOCUS *(excludes binding)*	DEEP PURPLE	1⅛ yds	⅞ yd	¾ yd	½ yd	⅜ yd	
COMPANION	PURPLE	½ yd	⅜ yd	¼ yd		¼ yd	⅛ yd
ZINGER *(includes inner border)*	ORANGE BATIK	¾ yd	½ yd	⅜ yd	¼ yd	⅛ yd	
RING	PURPLE w/ ORANGE	1⅛ yds	⅞ yd	⅝ yd	½ yd	⅜ yd	¼ yd
SETTING BLOCKS AND EXTENSION	SHIBORI	2⅜ yd	2 yds	1 yd		½ yd	
BORDER	PURPLE PRINT	4¾ yds	3¾ yds	1⅞ yds	1½ yds	1¼ yds	⅞ yd
LEMOYNE STARS *(may just add ⅛ yd to Crisscross fabric if you use the same fabric)*	RAINBOW GRADATION						
(lightest)	BUTTER YELLOW	¼ yd	not used	⅛ yd	not used	⅛ yd	not used
	YELLOW						
	YELLOW-ORANGE						
	ORANGE						
	RED-ORANGE	¼ yd		⅛ yd		⅛ yd	
	RED						
	MAGENTA-RED						
	RED-MAGENTA						
	MAGENTA						
(darkest)	PURPLE-MAGENTA	¼ yd	not used	⅛ yd	not used	⅛ yd	not used
BINDING *(may add to Focus fabric)*	DEEP PURPLE	⅞ yd		⅜ yd		¼ yd	

FINISHED SIZES	LARGE		MEDIUM		MINIATURE	
	5R	4R (shown)	5R	4R	5R	4R
QUILT (includes binding)	91" x 109½"	76¾" x 97"	48¾" x 58¾"	40⅝" x 50⅜"	28¼" x 33¾"	22½" x 27½"
LEMOYNE STAR BLOCK	8½" x 8½"	8½" x 8½"	4¼" x 4¼"	4¼" x 4¼"	2¼" x 2¼"	2¼" x 2¼"
PINEAPPLE STAR WITH EXTENSION	54¼" x 72½"	45¼" x 65½"	29" x 39"	24⅛" x 33⅞"	14½" x 20"	12" x 18"

CUTTING GUIDES

Refer to the guides below and on pages 80–82 to cut the appropriate border, binding, and block pieces for your size quilt. Note that there are separate cutting guides on page 82 for the border containing the LeMoyne Star blocks. Refer to the guide on page 57 to cut the Pineapple Star setting blocks. In this design, the setting block fabric extends beyond the star at the top and bottom edges. The LeMoyne stars in the border use offset strips to create the staggered effect.

BORDER/BINDING CUTTING GUIDE	LARGE		MEDIUM		MINIATURE	
	5R	4R (shown)	5R	4R	5R	4R
BACKGROUND EXTENSION	Two 10⅛" x 55" (cut lengthwise)	Two 10⅝" x 46" (cut lengthwise)	Two 5⅛" x 29¾"	Two 5⅜" x 25"	Two 3¼" x 15"	Two 3½" x 12½"
INNER BORDER	7 strips 2½"	6 strips 1½"	4 strips 1½"	4 strips 1"	2 strips 1¼"	2 strips 1"
MIDDLE BORDER	8 strips 3½"	6 strips 1¾"	4 strips 2⅛"	4 strips 1"	3 strips 1⅞"	2 strips 1"
LEMOYNE STAR BORDER	see separate charts		see separate charts		see separate charts	
OUTER BORDER	11 strips 3½"	10 strips 3½"	6 strips 2½"	5 strips 2½"	4 strips 2¼"	3 strips 1¼"
BINDING	11 strips 2⅜"	10 strips 2⅜"	6 strips 1⅝"	5 strips 1⅝"	4 strips 1¼"	3 strips 1¼"

ASSEMBLY

1. Paper-piece 8 Diamond Pineapple blocks. (See Piecing the Block, pages 27–35.)

2. Join the blocks in a Star of Bethlehem. (See Piecing the Star, pages 38–43.)

3. Insert 4 square and 4 triangle setting blocks. (See Setting Blocks, pages 45–48.) Sew a background extension strip to the top and bottom edges of the star.

4. Join the side inner borders. Press. Add the top and bottom inner borders. Press. Add the side middle borders. Press. Add the top and bottom middle borders. Press. (See Classic Border, page 51.)

5. Join the small diamonds together to make a gradated set of LeMoyne Stars. Make 2 stars in your lightest color, 2 stars in your darkest color, and four stars of each remaining color. Insert the border fabric setting triangles and setting squares to complete each block. Make 36 blocks for a 5-round quilt, 28 blocks for a 4-round quilt.

6. Place the quilt top on a design wall or the floor. Center a lightest LeMoyne Star block on each side edge of the Pineapple Star unit. Center the darkest LeMoyne Star block on the top and bottom edges. Place the lightest Outer Crisscross LeMoyne Star blocks in the four corners. Arrange the remaining stars in between, for a gradated progression around the edges.

7. Sew an offset strip to one (top) edge of each LeMoyne Star block. Press. Add another offset strip to a side edge of the 4 corner blocks. Press. Return the blocks to the design wall. Turn every other block so that the offset strip is on the outside edge and the stars are staggered. In 4-round quilts, the middle star in the top and bottom borders will be closer to the quilt center and the side middle stars and corner blocks will be closer to the quilt edge. In 5-round quilts, the middle star in the top and bottom borders will be closer to the edge. On the sides, middle stars and corner blocks will be closer to the quilt center. Place spacing strips between the stars. Sew the pieces together to make 2 side LeMoyne Star borders and top and bottom LeMoyne Star borders. Press.

4R	STAR SIZE		LARGE (45¼")			MEDIUM (24⅛")			MINIATURE (12")		
FABRIC	POSITION	#	WIDTH	STRIP	SUBCUT	WIDTH	STRIP	SUBCUT	WIDTH	STRIP	SUBCUT
CENTER DIAMOND	#1	8	6"	1	3"	3⅜"	1	1¾"	2"	1	1¼"
INNER CRISSCROSS FABRICS											
STEP 6	#2 I			2	4¼"	1¼"	1	2½"	1"	1	1½"
STEP 7	#4 I	16	1¾"		5"			3"			1¾"
STEP 8	#6 I			3	5¾"		2	3½"			2"
STEP 9	#8 I				6½"			4"			2¼"
OUTER CRISSCROSS STEP 5	#2 O			2	4¼"		1	2½"			1½"
STEP 4	#4 O	16	1¾"		5"	1¼"		3"	1"	1	1¾"
STEP 3	#6 O			3	5¾"		2	3½"			2"
STEP 2	#8 O				6½"			4"			2¼"
FOCUS FABRIC *(Outer plus both Triangles)*	#3 S (O)			1	3"			1¾"			1¼"
	#5 S (O)	8	1¾"		4¼"	1¼"	1	2½"	1"	1	1½"
	#7 S (O)			2	5½"			3⅛"			2"
	#9 S (O)				6¾"			3¾"			2¼"
	#11 triangle	16	8"	2	6⅝"	5"	1	4⅛"	3⅛"	1	2⅝"
COMPANION FABRIC *(Inner)*	#3 S (I)			1	3"			1¾"			1¼"
	#5 S (I)	8	1¾"		4¼"	1¼"	1	2½"	1"	1	1½"
	#7 S (I)			2	5½"			3⅛"			2"
ZINGER	#9 S (I)	8	1¾"	2	6¾"	1¼"	1	3¾"	1"	1	2¼"
RING FABRIC	#3 L			3	6¼"			4¼"			2"
	#5 L				6¾"		2	4½"		1	2¼"
	#7 L	16	1¾"	4	7¼"	1¼"		4¾"	1"		2⅜"
	#9 L				7¾"			5"		2	3"
	#11 L			2*	3½"		2*	2¾"		1*	2"

** Use leftovers from previous strips*

8. Join the side LeMoyne Star borders to the quilt top. Press. Join the corner blocks to the top and bottom LeMoyne Star borders. Press. Add these borders to the quilt top. Add the side outer borders to the quilt top. Press. Add the top and bottom outer borders to the quilt top. Press.

9. To replicate the project quilt, add free-motion embroidery to the quilt top.

10. Layer and finish the quilt. (See Quilting, pages 53–55.) The project quilt has free-motion quilting.

5R / FABRIC	STAR SIZE / POSITION	#	LARGE (54¼") WIDTH	STRIP	SUBCUT	MEDIUM (29") WIDTH	STRIP	SUBCUT	MINIATURE (14½") WIDTH	STRIP	SUBCUT
CENTER DIAMOND	#1	8	6"	1	3"	3⅜"	1	1¾"	2"	1	1¼"
INNER CRISSCROSS FABRICS	*(rainbow gradation with 10 steps, with #1 being the darkest and #10 being the lightest)*										
STEP 6	#2 I			2	4¼"		1	2½"			1½"
STEP 7	#4 I				5"			3"			1¾"
STEP 8	#6 I	16	1¾"	3	5¾"	1¼"	2	3½"	1"	1	2"
STEP 9	#8 I				6½"			4"			2¼"
STEP 10	#10 I			4	7¾"			4½"			2½"
OUTER CRISSCROSS STEP 5	#2 O			2	4¼"		1	2½"			1½"
STEP 4	#4 O				5"			3"			1¾"
STEP 3	#6 O	16	1¾"	3	5¾"	1¼"	2	3½"	1"	1	2"
STEP 2	#8 O				6½"			4"			2¼"
STEP 1	#10 O			4	7¾"			4½"			2½"
FOCUS FABRIC *(Outer plus both Triangles)*	#3 S (O)			1	3"			1¾"			1¼"
	#5 S (O)				4¼"			2½"			1½"
	#7 S (O)	8	1¾"		5½"	1¼"	1	3⅛"	1"	1	2"
	#9 S (O)			2	6¾"			3¾"			2¼"
	#11 S (O)				8¼"			4⅝"			2½"
	#13 Triangle	16	9½"	2	7⅞"	5⅞"	2	4⅞"	3½"	1	2⅞"
COMPANION FABRIC *(Inner)*	#3 S (I)			1	3"			1¾"			1¼"
	#5 S (I)	8	1¾"		4¼"	1¼"	1	2½"	1"	1	1½"
	#7 S (I)			2	5½"			3⅛"			2"
	#9 S (I)				6¾"			3¾"			2¼"*
ZINGER	#11 S (I)	8	1¾"	2	8¼"	1¼"	1	4⅝"	1"	1	2½"
RING FABRIC	#3 L			3	6¼"			4¼"			2"
	#5 L				6¾"		2	4½"		1	2¼"
	#7 L	16	1¾"		7¼"	1¼"		4¾"	1"		2⅜"
	#9 L			4	7¾"			5"			2½"
	#11 L				8½"		3	5¼"		2	3"
	#13 L			2*	3½"		2*	2¾"		1*	2"

Use leftovers from previous strips

5R LEYMOYNE STAR BORDER

FABRIC	STAR SIZE	LARGE				MEDIUM				MINIATURE			
LIGHTEST AND DARKEST RAINBOW	DIAMOND	2¼"	2	2¼", 45°	16 each	1⅜"	1	1⅜", 45°	16 each	1"	1	1", 45°	16 each
REMAINING RAINBOW COLORS	DIAMOND	2¼"	3	2¼", 45°	32 each	1⅜"	2	1⅜", 45°	32 each	1"	2	1", 45°	32 each
BORDER	SETTING SQUARE	3"	12	3"	144	1¾"	5	1¾"	144	1⅛"	4*	1⅛"	144
	SETTING TRIANGLE	4¾"	5	4¾", subcut diagonally twice	36 squares (144 triangles)	3"	3	3", subcut diagonally twice	36 squares (144 triangles)	2¼"	3	2¼", subcut diagonally twice	36 squares (144 triangles)
	OFFSET STRIP	2¼"	9	9"	36		5	4¾"	36		3	3"	32
		2¼"	2	10¾"	4	1¼"	1	5½"	4	1"	1*	2¾"	4
	SPACER	1¼"	11		32		5		32		4	3½"	36

* Use leftovers from other border fabric strips

4R LEMOYNE STAR BORDER

FABRIC	POSITION	WIDTH	STRIP	SUBCUT	#	WIDTH	STRIP	SUBCUT	#	WIDTH	STRIP	SUBCUT	#
		LARGE				MEDIUM				MINIATURE			
LIGHTEST AND DARKEST RAINBOW	DIAMOND	2¼"	2	2¼", 45°	16 each	1⅜"	1	1⅜", 45°	16 each	1"	1	1", 45°	16 each
REMAINING RAINBOW COLORS	DIAMOND	2¼"	3	2¼", 45°	32 each	1⅜"	2	1⅜", 45°	32 each	1"	2	1", 45°	32 each
BORDER	SETTING SQUARE	3"	9	3"	112	1¾"	5	1¾"	112	1⅛"	4	1⅛"	112
	SETTING TRIANGLE	4¾"	4	4¾", subcut diagonally twice	28 squares (112 triangles)	3"	3	3", subcut diagonally twice	28 squares (112 triangles)	2¼"	2	2¼", subcut diagonally twice	28 squares (112 triangles)
	OFFSET STRIP		7	9"	28		3	4¾"	28		2	2¾"	24
	SPACER	2¼"	2*	10¾"	4	1¼"	1*	5½"	4	1"	1*	2¾"	4
			7		20		3		20		3	3"	28

* Use leftovers from other border fabric strips

School
Spirit

SHARON REXROAD, 2004
Quilted by Jan Sears.

STYLE: Stretched Star

DESIGN FEATURES: Fussy-cut tips, pieced setting blocks, embroidered center

EDGE: Piped binding

BLOCKS: 12 Diamond Pineapples, 5 pieced setting squares, 6 pieced setting triangles

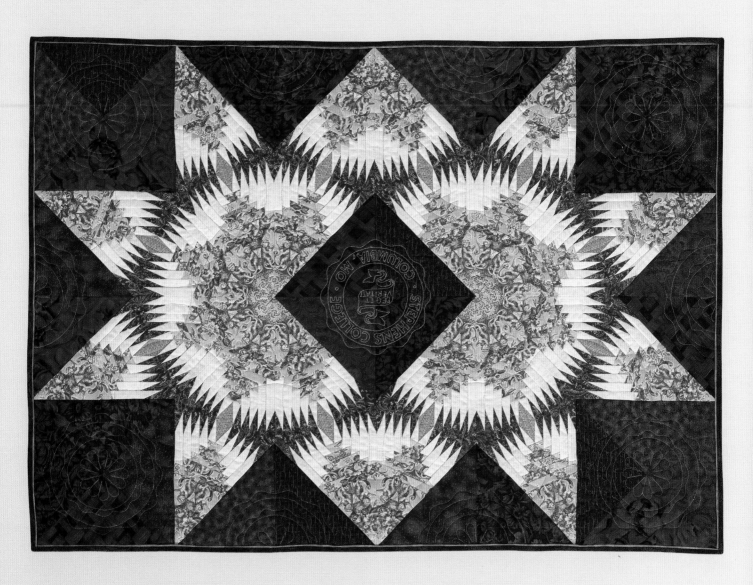

FINISHED SIZES	LARGE		MEDIUM		MINIATURE	
	5R (shown)	4R	5R	4R	5R	4R
QUILT (includes binding)	54¼" x 77½"	45¼" x 64¾"	29" x 41½"	24⅛" x 34⅝"	14½" x 20⅞"	12" x 17½"
PINEAPPLE STAR	54¼"	45¼"	29"	24⅛"	14½"	12"

FABRIC		LARGE		MEDIUM		MINIATURE	
		5R	4R	5R (shown)	4R	5R	4R
CENTER DIAMOND	BRIGHT GOLD	¼ yd		⅛ yd		⅛ yd	
CRISSCROSS	CREAM	2 yds	1½ yds	1 yd	⅔ yd	½ yd	⅜ yd
FOCUS	YELLOW/ RED TOILE	1½ yds	1¼ yds	⅞ yd	¾ yd	½ yd	⅜ yd
RING	DEEP RED/GOLD	1½ yds	1¼ yds	¾ yd	⅝ yd	½ yd	⅜ yd
SETTING BLOCKS	6 DEEP REDS	½ yd each		⅜ yd each	¼ yd each	¼ yd each	
PIPING (may add to Center Diamond fabric)	BRIGHT GOLD	¼ yd		⅛ yd		⅛ yd	
BINDING	DEEP RED	⅝ yd (8 strips 2⅜")	½ yd (6 strips 1⅜")	¼ yd (4 strips 1⅝")		⅛ yd (2 strips 1¼")	

CUTTING GUIDES

Refer to the guides on pages 85 and 86 to cut the appropriate Diamond Pineapple and setting block pieces for your size quilt. The setting blocks are pieced together from smaller triangles, enhancing the scrappy look of the quilt. Note that in the project quilt, 8 deep reds were used in the setting blocks. The fabric guide lists 6, for more efficient use of the fabrics.

4R	STAR SIZE		LARGE (45¼"x 64¾")			MEDIUM (24⅛"x 35")			MINIATURE (12"x 17½")		
FABRIC	POSITION	#	WIDTH	STRIP	SUBCUT	WIDTH	STRIP	SUBCUT	WIDTH	STRIP	SUBCUT
CENTER DIAMOND	#1	12	6"	1	3"	3⅜"	1	1¾"	2"	1	1¼"
CRISSCROSS	#2 I+O				4¼"		3	2½"		2	1½"
	#4 I+O	48	1¾"	6	5"	1¼"	4	3"	1"		1¾"
	#6 I+O				5¾"		5	3½"		3	2"
	#8 I+O			7	6½"			4"			2¼"
FOCUS FABRIC	#3 S			2	3"			1¾"		1	1¼"
	#5 S		1¾"	3	4¼"	1¼"	2	2½"	1"		1½"
	#7 S	24		4	5½"			3⅛"		2	2"
	#9 S				6¾"		3	3¾"			2¼"
FUSSY CUT	#11 Triangle		8"	3	6⅝"	5"	2	4⅛"	3⅛"	1	2⅝"
RING FABRIC	#3 L			4	6¼"			4¼"			2"
	#5 L				6¾"		3	4½"			2¼"
	#7 L	24	1¾"	5	7¼"	1¼"		4¾"	1"	2	2⅜"
	#9 L				7¾"			5"			2½"
	#11 L			3	3½"		2	2¾"			2"

5R	STAR SIZE		LARGE (54¼"x 77¼")			MEDIUM (29"x 41¾")			MINIATURE (14½"x 22⅛")		
FABRIC	POSITION	#	WIDTH	STRIP	SUBCUT	WIDTH	STRIP	SUBCUT	WIDTH	STRIP	SUBCUT
CENTER DIAMOND	#1	12	6"	1	3"	3⅜"	1	1¾"	2"	1	1¼"
CRISSCROSS	#2 I+O			6	4¼"		3	2½"		2	1½"
	#4 I+O				5"		4	3"			1¾"
	#6 I+O	48	1¾"	7	5¾"	1¼"	5	3½"	1"	3	2"
	#8 I+O			8	6½"			4"			2¼"
	#10 I+O			10	7¾"		6	4½"			2½"
FOCUS FABRIC	#3 S			2	3"			1¾"		1	1¼"
	#5 S			3	4¼"		2	2½"			1½"
	#7 S	24	1¾"	4	5½"	1¼"		3⅛"	1"		2"
	#9 S				6¾"		3	3¾"		2	2¼"
	#11 S			6	8¼"			4⅝"			2½"
FUSSY CUT	#13 Triangle		9½"	3	7⅞"	5⅞"	2	4⅞"	3½"	1	2⅞"
RING FABRIC	#3 L			4	6¼"			4¼"			2"
	#5 L				6¾"		3	4½"			2¼"
	#7 L	24	1¾"	5	7¼"	1¼"		4¾"	1"	2	2⅜"
	#9 L				7¾"			5"			2½"
	#11 L			6	8¼"		4	5¼"			3"
	#13 L			3	3½"		2	2¾"			2"

SETTING BLOCKS CUTTING GUIDE	LARGE		MEDIUM		MINIATURE	
	5R	4R	5R (shown)	4R	5R	4R (shown)
PIECED SQUARE BLOCKS: Cut 5 A squares. Subcut diagonally in both directions for 20 A triangles	17¼" x 17¼"	4⅝" " x 14⅝"	9⅞" x 9⅞"	8⅜" x 8⅜"	5½" x 5½"	4⅞" x 4⅞"
PIECED TRIANGLE BLOCKS: Cut 6 B squares. Subcut diagonally in half for 12 B triangles	12¼" x 12¼"	10⅜" x 10⅜"	7" x 7" square	6" x 6"	4" x 4"	3½" x 3½"

ASSEMBLY

1. Paper-piece 12 Diamond Pineapple blocks. (See Piecing the Block, pages 27–35.)

2. Join the blocks into sections of a Stretched Star. (See Piecing the Star, pages 38–43.)

3. Piece 4 A triangles together on the shorter bias edges to make a square block; take care not to stretch the bias edges when sewing. Press seams open. Make 5 setting squares. Piece 2 B triangles together on the shorter straight-grain edges to make a larger triangle. Press seams open. Make 6 setting triangles.

4. Insert the setting triangles and squares into the Stretched Star sections. Join sections in sequence until the Stretched Star is complete. (See Setting Blocks, pages 45–48.)

5. Layer and finish the quilt. (See Quilting, pages 53–55.) This quilt has curved quilting over the diamond pineapple blocks and a machine embroidered logo in the center square. Stephens College, a small professional, peforming, and liberal arts women's college in Missouri (and my alma mater) graciously granted permission for Bernina-USA to digitize the school logo for use on this quilt. The embroidery was done on an Artista 200E machine. Remaining setting blocks are quilted in a design to complement the embroidered design.

6. From piping fabric, cut ¾"-wide strips. Piece strips as needed to make one continuous strip for each side of your quilt. Press each strip in half, right sides out. Baste a piping strip to each edge, then secure it in the binding seam.

Shake Rattle & Roll

SHARON REXROAD, 2000

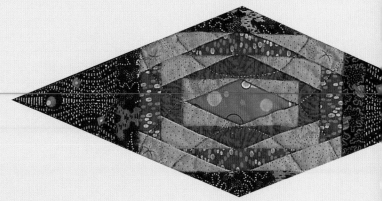

STYLE: Rolling Star

DESIGN FEATURES: Rainbowing, fussy-cut tips, interior zinger strips

EDGE: Simple border

BLOCKS: 32 Diamond Pineapples, 12 setting squares, 8 setting triangles, 4 setting rectangles

Note that this quilt is made with 3R blocks. The project directions are for 4R or 5R blocks.

FINISHED SIZES	LARGE		MEDIUM		MINIATURE	
	5R	4R	5R	4R	5R	4R
QUILT(*includes binding*)	113" x 113"	95" x 95"	60½" x 60½"	50¾" x 50¾"	30½" x 30½"	25½" x 25½"
PINEAPPLE BLOCK	54¼"	45¼"	29"	24⅛"	14½"	12"

		LARGE		MEDIUM		MINIATURE	
		5R	4R	5R	4R	5R	4R
CENTER DIAMOND	RED PRINT	¾ yd		⅜ yd		⅛ yd	
CRISSCROSS	LIME GREEN	5⅛ yds	3¾ yds	2⅜ yds	1¾ yds	1⅛ yds	⅞ yd
FOCUS (*combine with Ring fabric*)	BRIGHTEST BLUE	⅜ yd		¼ yd each		⅛ yd each	
	BRIGHT BLUE	½ yd					
	BLUE	⅝ yd					
	BLUE WITH BLACK	¾ yd	½ yd	⅜ yd	¼ yd	¼ yd	⅛ yd
	BLACK WITH BLUE	½ yd	1½ yds	¼ yd	¾ yd	⅛ yd	⅜ yd
	BLACK-BASED	2⅜ yds	not used	1 yd	not used	½ yd	not used
ZINGER	RED/BLACK PRINT	½ yd	⅜ yd	¼ yd		⅛ yd	
RING (*combine with Focus fabric*)	BRIGHTEST BLUE	¾ yd each		½ yd each		¼ yd each	
	BRIGHT BLUE						
	BLUE						
	BLUE WITH BLACK						
	BLACK WITH BLUE	1 yd	½ yd	½ yd	¼ yd		
	BLACK-BASED	½ yd	not used	¼ yd	not used	¼ yd	not used
SETTING BLOCKS	SOLID BLACK	5⅝ yds	4⅝ yds	1¾ yds	1¼ yds	⅝ yd	½ yd
BORDER (*may add to Zinger fabric*)	RED/BLACK PRINT	1 yd	⅞ yd	⅜ yd		⅛ yd	
BINDING (*may add to Center Diamond fabric*)	RED PRINT	⅞ yd		⅜ yd		¼ yd	

CUTTING GUIDES

Refer to the guides below and on page 90 to cut the appropriate border, binding, and block pieces for your size quilt. Refer to the guide on page 57 to cut the setting blocks.

BORDER/BINDING CUTTING GUIDE	LARGE		MEDIUM		MINIATURE	
	5R	4R	5R	4R	5R	4R
BORDERS	12 strips 2½"	10 strips 2½"	6 strips 1½"	6 strips 1½"	4 strips 1"	4 strips 1"
BINDING	13 strips 2⅜"	11 strips 2⅜"	7 strips 1⅝"	6 strips 1⅝"	4 strips 1¼"	3 strips 1¼"

4R	STAR SIZE	#	LARGE (45¼")			MEDIUM (24⅛")			MINIATURE (12")		
FABRIC	POSITION	#	WIDTH	STRIP	SUBCUT	WIDTH	STRIP	SUBCUT	WIDTH	STRIP	SUBCUT
CENTER DIAMOND	#1	32	6"	3	3"	3⅜"	2	1¾"	2"	1	1¼"
CRISSCROSS #2 I+O				15	4¼"		8	2½"		5	1½"
#4 I+O		128	1¾"	16	5"	1¼"	10	3"	1"	6	1¾"
#6 I+O				19	5¾"		12	3½"		7	2"
#8 I+O				22	6½"		13	4"		8	2¼"
FOCUS FABRICS *(gradation)*											
BRIGHTEST BLUE	#3 S			5	3"		3	1¾"		2	1¼"
BRIGHT BLUE	#5 S	64	1¾"	8	4¼"	1¼"	4	2½"	1"	3	1½"
BLUE	#7 S			10	5½"		6	3⅛"		4	2"
BLUE WITH BLACK	#9 S (O)	32		6	6¾"		4	3¾"		2	2¼"
BLACK WITH BLUE *(fussy cut)*	#11 Triangle	64	8"	6	6⅝"	5"	4	4⅛"	3⅛"	3	2⅝"
ZINGER *(Inner)*	#9 S (I)	32	1¾"	6	6¾"	1¼"	4	3¾"	1"	2	2¼"
RING FABRICS *(gradation)*											
BRIGHTEST BLUE	#3 L			11	6¼"			4¼"			2"
BRIGHT BLUE	#5 L				6¾"		8	4½"		4	2¼"
BLUE	#7 L	64	1¾"	13	7¼"	1¼"		4¾"	1"		2⅜"
BLUE WITH BLACK	#9 L				7¾"			5"		5	3"
BLACK WITH BLUE	#11 L			6	3½"		5	2¾"		4	2"

1. Paper-piece 32 Diamond Pineapple blocks. (See Piecing the Block, pages 27–35.) On each round, use the same fabrics for both the focus fabric and the ring fabric positions.

2. Join the blocks into sections of a Rolling Star. (See Piecing the Star, pages 38–44.)

3. Insert the setting blocks into Rolling Star sections. Continue joining blocks and sections in sequence until the Rolling Star is complete. (See Setting Blocks, pages 45–47 and 49–50.)

4. Add the side borders and the top and bottom borders to the quilt top. (See Classic Borders, page 51.)

5. Layer and finish the quilt. (See Quilting, pages 53–55.) The project quilt has curved quilting lines in the setting blocks, to suggest old 45 rpm records. Quilted lettering in the rectangle setting blocks spells out the quilt name.

5R	STAR SIZE		LARGE (54¼")			MEDIUM (29")			MINIATURE (14½")		
FABRIC	**POSITION**	**#**	**WIDTH**	**STRIP**	**SUBCUT**	**WIDTH**	**STRIP**	**SUBCUT**	**WIDTH**	**STRIP**	**SUBCUT**
CENTER DIAMOND	#1	32	6"	3	3"	3⅜"	2	1¾"	2"	1	1¼"
CRISSCROSS	#2 I+O			15	4¼"		8	2½"		5	1½"
	#4 I+O			16	5"		10	3"		6	1¾"
	#6 I+O	128	1¾"	19	5¾"	1¼"	12	3½"	1"	7	2"
	#8 I+O			22	6½"		13	4"		8	2¼"
	#10 I+O			26	7¾"		16	4½"			2½"
FOCUS FABRICS (gradation)											
BRIGHTEST BLUE	#3 S			5	3"		3	1¾"		2	1¼"
BRIGHT BLUE	#5 S	64		8	4¼"		4	2½"		3	1½"
BLUE	#7 S		1¾"	10	5½"	1¼"	6	3⅛"	1"	4	2"
BLUE WITH BLACK	#9 S			11	6¾"		7	3¾"			2¼"
BLACK WITH BLUE (Outer)	#11 S (O)	32		8	8¼"		4	4⅝"		2	2½"
BLACK BASED (Fussy Cut)	#13 Triangle	64	9½"	8	7⅞"	5⅞"	5	4⅞"	3½"	3	2⅞"
ZINGER (Inner)	#11 S (I)	32	1¾"	8	8¼"	1¼"	4	4⅝"	1"	2	2½"
RING FABRICS (gradation)											
BRIGHTEST BLUE	#3 L			11	6¼"			4¼"			2"
BRIGHT BLUE	#5 L				6¾"			4½"		4	2¼"
BLUE	#7 L	64	1¾"	13	7¼"	1¼"	8	4¾"	1"		2⅜"
BLUE WITH BLACK	#9 L				7¾"			5"			2½"
BLACK WITH BLUE	#11 L			16	8¼"		10	5¼"		5	3"
BLACK BASED	#13 L			6	3½"		5	2¾"		4	2"

New Day Dawning

SHARON REXROAD, 2001
Quilted by Jan Sears

STYLE: Broken Star

DESIGN FEATURES: Light to dark gradation, fussy-cut center, zinger strips

EDGE: Binding

BLOCKS: 32 Diamond Pineapples, 12 setting squares, 8 setting triangles, 4 setting rectangles

FINISHED SIZES	LARGE		MEDIUM		MINIATURE	
	5R (shown)	4R	5R	4R	5R	4R
QUILT (includes binding)	109¼" x 109¼"	91¼" x 91¼"	58½" x 58½"	48¾" x 48¾"	29⅜" x 29⅜"	24½" x 24½"
PINEAPPLE STAR	54¼"	45¼"	29"	24⅛"	14½"	12"

		LARGE		MEDIUM		MINIATURE	
		5R (shown)	4R	5R	4R	5R	4R
CENTER DIAMOND	RED MARBLE	¾ yd		⅜ yd		⅛ yd	
CRISSCROSS (10-step gradation)							
PALEST	PALEST BLUE	¾ yd	not used	⅜ yd	not used	¼ yd	not used
	PALE BLUE	⅝ yd		⅜ yd		¼ yd	
	LIGHT BLUE						
	MEDIUM-LIGHT BLUE	½ yd		¼ yd		⅛ yd	
	MEDIUM BLUE						
	MEDIUM DARK BLUE						
	DARK BLUE						
	DEEP BLUE	⅝ yd		⅜ yd		¼ yd	
	DEEPER BLUE						
DEEPEST	DEEPEST BLUE	¾ yd	not used	⅜ yd	not used	¼ yd	not used
FOCUS (more for fancy cuts)	FLORAL	4½ yds	3 yds	2 yds	1⅜ yds	⅞ yd	¾ yd
ZINGER	BLACK PRINT	½ yd		¼ yd		⅛ yd	
RING	YELLOW CHECK	3¾ yds	3 yds	1¾ yds	1⅜ yds	⅞ yd	¾ yd
SETTING BLOCKS	SOFT BUTTER	6½ yds	5 yds	1⅞ yds	1½ yds	¾ yd	⅝ yd
BINDING (may add to Center Diamond fabric)	RED MARBLE	1 yd 12 strips 2⅜"	¾ yd 10 strips 2⅜"	½ yd 7 strips1⅝"	⅜ yd 6 strips1⅝"	¼ yd 4 strips1¼"	¼ yd 3 strips1¼"

CUTTING GUIDES

Refer to the guides on pages 93 and 94 to cut the appropriate Diamond Pineapple block pieces for your size quilt. Refer to the guide on page 57 to cut the setting blocks.

ASSEMBLY

1. Paper-piece 32 Diamond Pineapple blocks. (See Piecing the Block, pages 27–35.) Sew the gradated crisscross strips with the medium and medium dark colors in position #2. The colors at the inner end of the block become progressively lighter as you move toward the block edges, and progressively darker at the outer end of the block.

4R	STAR SIZE		LARGE (45⅝")			MEDIUM (24¾")			MINIATURE (12⅜")		
FABRIC	POSITION	#	WIDTH	STRIP	SUBCUT	WIDTH	STRIP	SUBCUT	WIDTH	STRIP	SUBCUT
CENTER DIAMOND	#1	32	6"	3	3"	3⅜"	2	1¾"	2"	1	1¼"
CRISSCROSS FABRICS *(light to dark gradation)*											
MEDIUM*	#2 I				4¼"		4	2½"			1½"
MEDIUM-DARK	#2 O			8						3	
MEDIUM-LIGHT	#4 I				5"		5	3"			1¾"
DARK	#4 O	64	1¾"			1¼"			1"		
LIGHT	#6 I			10	5¾"		6	3½"			2"
DEEP	#6 O									4	
PALE	#8 I			11	6½"		7	4"			2¼"
DEEPER	#8 O										
FOCUS FABRIC	#3 S			5	3"		3	1¾"		2	1¼"
	#5 S	64	1¾"	8	4¼"	1¼"	4	2½"	1"	3	1½"
	#7 S			10	5½"		6	3⅛"		4	2"
(Outer Only)	#9 S O	32		6	6¾"		4	3¾"		2	2¼"
(Fussy Cut)	#11 Triangle	64	8"	6	6⅝"	5"		4⅛"	3⅛"	3	2⅝"
ZINGER FABRIC	#9 S I	32	1¾"	6	6¾"	1¼"	4	3¾"	1"	2	2¼"
RING FABRIC	#3 L			11	6¼"			4¼"		4	2"
	#5 L				6¾"		8	4½"			2¼"
	#7 L	64	1¾"	13	7¼"	1¼"		4¾"	1"	5	2⅜"
	#9 L				7¾"			5"			3"
	#11 L			6	3½"		5	2¾"		4	2"

2. Join the blocks into sections of a Broken Star. (See Piecing the Star, pages 38–43.)

3. Insert the setting blocks into the Broken Star sections. Sew sections in sequence until the Broken Star is complete. (See Setting Blocks, pages 45–49.)

4. Layer and finish the quilt. (See Quilting, pages 53–55.) This project quilt has curved quilting in the Diamond Pineapple blocks and machine trapunto in the setting blocks.

Trapunto quilting design from Hari Walner's Trapunto by Machine *(C&T Publishing, 1996).*

4R	STAR SIZE		LARGE (45¼")			MEDIUM (24⅛")			MINIATURE (12")		
FABRIC	POSITION	#	WIDTH	STRIP	SUBCUT	WIDTH	STRIP	SUBCUT	WIDTH	STRIP	SUBCUT
CENTER DIAMOND	#1	32	6"	3	3"	3⅜"	2	1¾"	2"	1	1¼"
CRISSCROSS FABRICS (light to dark gradation)											
MEDIUM	#2 I				4¼"		4	2½"			1½"
MEDIUM-DARK	#2 O			8						3	
MEDIUM-LIGHT	#4 I				5"		5	3"			1¾"
DARK	#4 O										
LIGHT	#6 I	64	1¾"	10	5¾"	1¼"	6	3½"	1"		2"
DEEP	#6 O										
PALE	#8 I			11	6½"		7	4"		4	2¼"
DEEPER	#8 O										
PALEST	#10 I			13	7¾"		8	4½"			2½"
DEEPEST	#10 O										
FOCUS FABRIC	#3 S			5	3"		3	1¾"		2	1¼"
	#5 S	64		8	4¼"		4	2½"		3	1½"
	#7 S		1¾"	10	5½"	1¼"	6	3⅛"	1"	4	2"
	#9 S			11	6¾"		7	3¾"			2¼"
(Outer Only)	#11 S Outer	32		8	8¼"		4	4⅝"		2	2½"
(Fancy Cut)	#13 Triangle	64	9½"	8	7⅞"	5⅞"	5	4⅞"	3½"	3	2⅞"
ZINGER FABRIC	#11 S Inner	32	1¾"	8	8¼"	1¼"	4	4⅝"	1"	2	2½"
RING FABRIC	#3 L			11	6¼"			4¼"		4	2"
	#5 L				6¾"		8	4½"			2¼"
	#7 L	64	1¾"	13	7¼"	1¼"		4¾"	1"	5	2⅜"
	#9 L				7¾"			5"			2½"
	#11 L			16	8¼"		10	5¼"			3"
	#13 L			6	3½"		5	2¾"		4	2"

Pineapple Stars Paper Piecing Patterns

C&T offers a special set of paper-piecing patterns to use with Sharon Rexroad's book *Pineapple Stars.* You receive 9 diamond block patterns (8 blocks for a star plus 1 extra for practice) in three different sizes—a total of 27 block patterns in all!

To order, call 1.800.284.1114 or visit the website at www.ctpub.com

ABOUT THE AUTHOR

It all started in childhood, when Sharon fought with her sister as to who got to sleep under which of their grandmother's quilts. As an adult, Sharon Rexroad is an award-winning quilter, respected teacher and author, and recipient of a Nebraska Arts Council Individual Artist Fellowship. Sharon's quilts have won three NQA awards and been juried into multiple AQS and IQA shows. Five of her quilts have been on magazine covers, most notably *Diamond Pineapple #8: Faerie Ring* in *Quilter's Newsletter Magazine* (April 1999) and *Perennial Friends* in *McCall's Quick Quilts* (May 2001). Sharon presented her unique Doily Magic method with huge success on HGTV's *Simply Quilts.* She enjoys teaching at guilds and conferences such as International Quilt Festival. She is known for her sense of color, a willingness to share her secrets, her humorous view of life as a quilt designer, and her ability to draw out the best from each student. Sharon invites readers to visit her website, www.sharonrexroad.com.

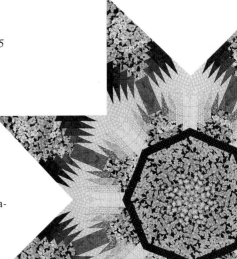